MW00355796

Bayard Rustin

The African American History Series

Series Editors:
Jacqueline M. Moore, Austin College, and Nina Mjagkij, Ball State University

Traditionally, history books tend to fall into two categories: books academics write for each other, and books written for popular audiences. Historians often claim that many of the popular authors do not have the proper training to interpret and evaluate the historical evidence. Yet, popular audiences complain that most historical monographs are inaccessible because they are too narrow in scope or lack an engaging style. This series, which will take both chronological and thematic approaches to topics and individuals crucial to an understanding of the African American experience, is an attempt to address that problem. The books in this series, written in lively prose by established scholars, are aimed primarily at nonspecialists. They focus on topics in African American history that have broad significance and place them in their historical context. While presenting sophisticated interpretations based on primary sources and the latest scholarship, the authors tell their stories in a succinct manner, avoiding jargon and obscure language. They include selected documents that allow readers to judge the evidence for themselves and to evaluate the authors' conclusions. Bridging the gap between popular and academic history, these books bring the African American story to life.

Volumes Published

Booker T. Washington, W.E.B. Du Bois, and the Struggle for Racial Uplift
Jacqueline M. Moore

Slavery in Colonial America, 1619–1776
Betty Wood

African Americans in the Jazz Age
A Decade of Struggle and Promise
Mark Robert Schneider

A. Philip Randolph
A Life in the Vanguard
Andrew E. Kersten

The African American Experience in Vietnam
Brothers in Arms
James Westheider

Bayard Rustin
American Dreamer
Jerald Podair

African Americans Confront Lynching
Strategies of Resistance
Christopher Waldrep

Lift Every Voice
The History of African American Music
Bruton W. Peretti

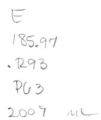
ROWMAN & LITTLEFIELD PUBLISHERS, INC.

Published in the United States of America
by Rowman & Littlefield Publishers, Inc.
A wholly owned subsidiary of The Rowman & Littlefield Publishing Group, Inc.
4501 Forbes Boulevard, Suite 200, Lanham, Maryland 20706
www.rowmanlittlefield.com

Estover Road
Plymouth PL6 7PY
United Kingdom

British Library Cataloguing in Publication Information Available

Library of Congress Cataloging-in-Publication Data

Podair, Jerald E., 1953–
  Bayard Rustin : American dreamer / Jerald Podair.
    p. cm. — (African American history series)
  ISBN-13: 978-0-7425-4513-7 (cloth : alk. paper)
  ISBN-10: 0-7425-4513-X (cloth)
  eISBN-13: 978-0-7425-6480-0
  eISBN-10: 0-7425-6480-0
  1. Rustin, Bayard, 1912-1987. 2. African Americans—Biography. 3. African American
civil rights workers—Biography. 4. African American pacifists—Biography. 5. African
American gay men—Biography. 6. African Americans—Civil rights. 7. Civil rights
movements—United States—History—20th century. 8. Nonviolence—United States—
History—20th century. 9. March on Washington for Jobs and Freedom, Washington, D.C.,
1963. I. Title.
  E185.97.R93P63 2009
  323.092—dc22
  [B]   2008025176

Printed in the United States of America

⊚™ The paper used in this publication meets the minimum requirements of American
National Standard for Information Sciences—Permanence of Paper for Printed Library
Materials, ANSI/NISO Z39.48-1992.

Bayard Rustin

American Dreamer

Jerald Podair

ROWMAN & LITTLEFIELD PUBLISHERS, INC.
Lanham • Boulder • New York • Toronto • Plymouth, UK

For Simon and Selma Podair

Contents

~

Chronology

March 17, 1912:	Bayard Rustin born in West Chester, Pennsylvania, to Florence Rustin. Raised by maternal grandparents Janifer and Julia Rustin.
Spring 1932:	Graduates from West Chester High School with honors.
September 1932:	Receives music scholarship to Wilberforce University in western Ohio.
1934:	Drops out of Wilberforce. Enrolls at Cheyney State Teachers College, a Quaker-founded school for black students.
1936:	Officially declares himself a Quaker and pacifist.
Fall 1937:	Moves from West Chester to New York City, just shy of graduating from Cheyney State.
1940:	Joins Young Communist League (YCL).
Winter– Spring 1941:	Works with socialist and labor leader A. Philip Randolph to plan March on Washington Movement against racial discrimination in defense industries.
June 1941:	After President Franklin Roosevelt issues Executive Order 8802 banning discrimination in war-related industries and establishing a Fair Employment Practice Committee to monitor compliance, Randolph cancels March on Washington.
Summer 1941:	YCL directs Rustin to cease activities on behalf of civil rights after the Soviet Union is attacked by Nazi Germany. He breaks with Communist Party.

September 1941:	Begins working for Fellowship of Reconciliation (FOR), a Christian pacifist organization.
1942:	FOR launches Congress of Racial Equality (CORE), a group dedicated to using nonviolent direct action to achieve racial integration in American society. Rustin becomes one of CORE's leaders and spokesmen.
January 1944:	Rustin is arrested for refusing to serve in U.S. military or accept alternative service as a conscientious objector.
February 1944:	Reports to a federal detention facility in Manhattan to begin serving sentence for avoiding draft. In March, he is transferred to a prison in Ashland, Kentucky.
1944–1946:	During his time in prison, Rustin organizes sit-ins and protests against racial segregation. The exposure of his homosexuality damages his relationship with FOR leaders. He is released from prison on June 11, 1946.
April 1947:	Rustin participates in the CORE-sponsored Journey of Reconciliation, which seeks to desegregate public transportation facilities in the upper South through nonviolent direct action.
1948:	Works with Randolph to end segregation in U.S. military.
July 1948:	President Harry Truman issues executive order prohibiting discrimination in the armed forces.
March–April 1949:	Rustin serves twenty-two days on a North Carolina chain gang after being convicted for engaging in civil disobedience during the Journey of Reconciliation.
January 1953:	After a speech in Pasadena, California, Rustin is arrested while engaging in sexual activity with two men. He is sentenced to prison and resigns from FOR.
March 1953:	Rustin is released from prison and returns to New York. In the fall, he accepts a position with the War Resisters League (WRL), a secular pacifist group.
February 1956:	Arrives in Montgomery, Alabama, to participate in Montgomery bus boycott. Mentors Martin Luther King, Jr., in the practice and philosophy of nonviolent direct action.
April 1956:	Rustin helps launch *Liberation* magazine, a journal of leftist ideas.
December 1956:	Montgomery boycott ends successfully with the desegregation of city's bus line.
December 1956– January 1957:	Participates in formation of Southern Christian Leadership Conference.

Spring 1958:	Travels to Europe for nuclear disarmament campaign.
June 1959:	Congressman Adam Clayton Powell, Jr., of New York publicly criticizes Rustin's influence on King. Privately, Powell threatens to spread rumors about a homosexual relationship between Rustin and King. King severs ties with Rustin.
December 1959– January 1960:	Rustin unsuccessfully attempts to halt a French nuclear testing in Algeria.
1961–1962:	Rustin engages in a series of debates with Nation of Islam leader Malcolm X.
December 1962:	Rustin and Randolph discuss possibility of the March on Washington for civil rights and economic justice.
Spring 1963:	King-led Birmingham civil rights campaign.
June 1963:	President John F. Kennedy announces he will send a civil rights bill to Congress.
July 1963:	Rustin and other civil rights leaders meet in Manhattan to begin planning the March on Washington for Jobs and Freedom.
July– August 1963:	Rustin takes lead role in organizing the March on Washington.
August 1963:	Senator Strom Thurmond of South Carolina attempts to discredit Rustin by exposing his homosexuality and communist past. Civil rights leaders come to Rustin's defense, and he remains in charge of the planning for the March on Washington.
August 28, 1963:	March on Washington for Jobs and Freedom is great success. King delivers "I Have a Dream" speech before interracial audience of 250,000.
February 1964:	Rustin organizes student and teacher boycott to protest racial segregation in New York City public schools.
July 1964:	Civil Rights Act passed.
August 1964:	Rustin urges Mississippi Freedom Democratic Party to accept Johnson administration's compromise proposal on seating its delegates at Democratic National Convention, angering many in the civil rights movement.
January 1965:	Rustin resigns from the WRL.
February 1965:	Publishes "From Protest to Politics: The Future of the Civil Rights Movement" in *Commentary*. A. Philip Randolph Institute founded, with Rustin as executive secretary.
August 1965:	Voting Rights Act passed.

October 1966:	Announces Freedom Budget and begins campaign to implement it.
April 4, 1968:	King assassinated in Memphis, Tennessee.
Spring–Fall 1968:	Becomes embroiled in the Ocean Hill-Brownsville school decentralization controversy in New York. His support for white-dominated United Federation of Teachers alienates city's black community.
October 1971:	Rustin suffers a heart attack. Recovers and continues his work.
1970s and 1980s:	Rustin works for Freedom House, a pro-democracy organization, and the International Rescue Committee, which assists refugees around the world.
1977:	Rustin meets Walter Naegle, who becomes his romantic partner for the rest of his life.
October 1984:	Rustin travels to New Haven, Connecticut, to support a strike by Yale's clerical and technical workers and is arrested.
1980s:	Encouraged by Walter Naegle, Rustin begins speaking out in favor of gay rights.
1985–1986:	Rustin lobbies New York City government officials on behalf of a gay rights bill, which is adopted.
July 1987:	Rustin and Naegle travel to Haiti to observe election processes. Upon returning to New York, Rustin falls ill.
August 24, 1987:	Rustin dies of heart failure in New York City at the age of 75.

~

Acknowledgments

My debts are many. I'm grateful to series editors Nina Mjagkij and Jacqueline Moore for asking the questions that challenged me to make this a better book. Thanks also to Niels Aaboe, Michelle Cassidy, Asa Johnson, Elaine McGarraugh, and Mary Bearden at Rowman & Littlefield, and to Robert Swanson.

Lawrence University is a most congenial and supportive place to teach and write. Special thanks to Provost David Burrows and to Joanne Johnson, two of our institution's greatest assets. I received much-appreciated financial assistance from Lawrence's Excellence in History Fund and from its Robert S. French Chair in American Studies. Thanks also to Corinne Wocelka of Lawrence's Seeley G. Mudd Library for arranging the acquisition of a microfilm edition of The Bayard Rustin Papers, aiding my work immeasurably. My research assistants, Alyson Richey and Caitlin Gallogly, both exemplary students at Lawrence, were indispensable to the process of writing this book. It would not exist without them.

Walter Naegle, Bayard Rustin's surviving partner, was extraordinarily generous with time, information, and resources, and gave me unique insights into the man he knew best. Andrew Kersten, whose volume on A. Philip Randolph is a stellar addition to this series, always offered me keen advice and wonderful friendship. Angenette Levy read this manuscript with care and used her sharp journalist's eye to save me from many errors. Jerry Seaman shared many meals with me at our favorite Appleton diner, patiently listening to me talk about this book. James McPherson remains an inspiration. I use what he taught me, and showed me, every day of my life as a historian.

I owe most of all to Caren and Julie Podair. I hope this book explains what I was doing in our basement the past two years.

∼

Shadow Man

Late in the afternoon of August 28, 1963, the day of the March on Washington for Jobs and Freedom, Bayard Rustin emerged from the shadows that had enveloped the first fifty-one years of his life. Martin Luther King, Jr., had just delivered the "I Have a Dream" speech, the words that would define the American civil rights movement, to an interracial audience of 250,000 gathered before the Lincoln Memorial. Now Rustin, the man who had organized the march, and whose decision it was to place King last on the list of speakers that day, stepped forward into the sunlight. Face glowing, arms thrust triumphantly in the air, he stood at the speakers' platform as the cheers of a quarter-million civil rights demonstrators washed over him. Few of the onlookers had heard of him before this afternoon, but they all knew him now. President John F. Kennedy, watching the proceedings on television a few blocks away at the White House, knew him, too. And when *Life* magazine, then the nation's cultural barometer, published its account of the march the following week, its cover photograph was not of King, but of Bayard Rustin.

Why did Bayard Rustin spend so much of his life in the shadows? The answer to this question lies initially in the details of his life. Rustin violated virtually every political and personal taboo in twentieth-century America. During the late 1930s and early 1940s, he was a member of the youth wing of the American Communist Party. After leaving its orbit, he spent the rest of his life as an active socialist. During World War II, he resisted the draft and spent over two years in federal prison. At the height of the Cold War he was an outspoken member of the pacifist movement, engaging in numerous acts of civil disobedience against the practices of the U.S. military. A civil rights activist since the

1930s, he had endured beatings, jail, and even time on a chain gang to challenge Jim Crow practices in the South, at a time when such protests went largely unrecognized in the North. And he was a homosexual who had been arrested in 1953, on what was known at the time as a "morals charge," an incident that exposed him to blackmail threats from opponents and rivals.

It is small wonder, given this background, that despite his charisma, courage, organizational abilities, rhetorical skills, and vision, Rustin was rarely permitted a leading public role in the social movements he helped shape. Civil rights leaders who relied heavily on his counsel and advice, including King, were nonetheless careful to keep him at arm's length. Rustin's turn for stardom on the speakers' podium at the March on Washington, then, was out of character for a man so familiar with life as an outsider, and whose undeniable talents were always freighted with heavy political and personal baggage.

Explaining Bayard Rustin's time in the shadows, however, involves more than surveying his tumultuous career. His life embodied the defining issues of the American national experience. What does "equality" mean in the United States? What is "freedom"? Americans have argued over these deceptively simple-sounding words—sometimes violently so—since the earliest days of the republic. Taken together, American understandings of "equality" and "freedom" have formed a larger vision, or dream, of what "America" meant as a nation and society. Rustin spent his life as a socialist, pacifist, civil rights activist, and homosexual struggling for his own version of that American dream of equality and freedom.

Rustin's dream owed much to those of other Americans. As an African American, he drew special inspiration from Thomas Jefferson's (1743–1826) assertion in the Declaration of Independence that "all men are created equal" and entitled equally to "life, liberty, and the pursuit of happiness." This language became the basis of his political and economic philosophy—his belief that every American was entitled to equal rights and an equal chance at the opportunities the nation offered.

The question of whether the words of the Declaration of Independence applied to African Americans, however, was not always a settled one. In its *Dred Scott v. Sanford* decision of 1857, the Supreme Court ruled that blacks were not citizens of the United States, and that the Declaration of Independence had not been intended to apply to them. Although the Fourteenth Amendment to the Constitution, ratified in 1868, overruled *Dred Scott* by making blacks federal citizens and prohibiting the denial of the equal protection of the laws and the taking of life, liberty, or property without due process of law, it still did not resolve the issue of equality, since another Supreme Court case, *Plessy v. Ferguson* (1896), defined the word "equal" to permit separate public accommodations for blacks and whites. And even the 1954 *Brown v. Board of Education* decision, in which the Court ruled that segregated public schools were "inherently unequal," was resisted in the South—and on a practical level, many parts of the North as well—during the decade leading up to the March on Washington. A major element of Rustin's dream, then, was animating the words of Thomas Jefferson in the America of the twentieth century.

Henry David Thoreau (1817–1862), whose 1846 essay "Civil Disobedience" argued that unjust laws could legitimately be violated in the interest of higher principles, was also one of Rustin's forerunners. Thoreau had refused to pay taxes to support the Mexican War, which he viewed as an attempt to extend slavery, and was sentenced to jail. He used his time in prison both to protest injustice and redeem himself through suffering. In Rustin's hands a century later, this form of protest would become nonviolent direct action, the philosophical and strategic engine of the modern civil rights movement. This aspect of Rustin's American dream invoked a moral code that enabled the weak to overcome the strong and to achieve justice through the power of the spirit.

Rustin's faith in democratic institutions reflected that of Abraham Lincoln (1809–1865). Like the sixteenth president, Rustin believed deeply in the ability of ordinary Americans to govern their own lives. He understood that a commitment to democracy often required equanimity in the face of grave disappointment. He refused to abandon that commitment even after suffering defeats that drove others to turn away from democratic politics in frustration and despair. Rustin spent the last decades of his life seeding democracy internationally by supervising elections in some of the world's most challenging venues. For him, as for Lincoln, democracy was less a strategy for attaining power than a cherished end in itself.

Walt Whitman (1819–1892) also shaped Rustin's American dream. Like Rustin, Whitman was a homosexual. His poetry evoked an ideal of individual fulfillment and self-expression that Rustin sought to realize in twentieth-century American life. Both men were willing to cross boundaries and challenge established behaviors in the cause of a uniquely American fellowship of free citizens. Rustin's humanitarianism—his desire to assist those he referred to as "people in trouble," regardless of their race or sexual orientation—reflected this quest for a true American community. Although Rustin did not actively pursue gay rights until relatively late in his career, his vision of an open and free nation in which personal and sexual choices were respected evoked that of Whitman.

Rustin's dream of an open and inclusive American community also borrowed from the early work of W. E. B. Du Bois (1868–1963). Du Bois assumed many personas during his long life—integrationist, Marxist, separatist, and, ultimately, expatriate—but he was always an advocate for the legal and political rights of African Americans. In *The Souls of Black Folk*, originally published in 1903, Du Bois wrote of his dream that it would one day be "possible for a man to be both a Negro and an American, without being cursed and spit upon by his

fellows, without having the doors of Opportunity closed roughly in his face."[1]
Du Bois's dream was pluralist and cosmopolitan. It envisioned a nation in which
all Americans could identify as Americans, while also honoring their racial,
ethnic, and religious affiliations. Rustin pursued these goals his entire life. His
commitment to racial integration never wavered over the course of a fifty-year
public career, continuing even as others retreated from it in the 1960s and
1970s. He did not seek an America in which race ceased to matter, but one in
which every American, in the words of Du Bois, could be "a co-worker in the
kingdom of culture," enriching the nation as a whole by permitting race to
"matter" only within a larger social and cultural framework.[2]

Rustin was an heir, finally, of Eugene V. Debs (1855–1926), America's preeminent socialist leader. In an era when radicalism in the United States was invariably derided as "foreign" in origin, Debs was a native-born original. He
sought to fuse political and economic democracy to soften the edges of a harsh
American industrial capitalism that ground workers' lives underfoot. He believed
that the United States could not be a truly "equal" nation as long as gross disparities in wealth and income existed. Rustin inherited this view of American
equality from Debs. He too wished to harness the power of American industry to
ensure a rough equivalence of economic condition for its citizens. Rustin believed that every American was entitled to a job, an income, an education, and
an adequate level of health care. And, like Debs, he believed in the power of organized labor to create an egalitarian America, both economically and, through
an alliance with the civil rights movement, politically and socially. To Rustin,
class and racial equality complemented each other in the struggle for equality
and freedom in the United States. Rustin believed that socialism could come to
America only through an interracial alliance of the working class and poor, and
he would make many sacrifices during his career in pursuit of this goal.

Bayard Rustin's American dream, then, was composed of elements borrowed
from others. But it was nonetheless uniquely his own. It was a dream rooted in
materialism in that it viewed "equality" in economic terms. But it also featured
a commitment to democratic practice, personal freedom, and individual conscience that distinguished it from Marxism. It married the ideas of economic
and racial equality to a communitarian ethos that bound together people of
plenty and "people in trouble." Above all, it was a dream rooted in humanism,
for Rustin's belief in individual dignity and worth, unlike many others on the
American left, was genuine. Rustin offered the hope of an American radicalism
that would challenge the nation to be true to its first principles.

By the time he stepped up to the speakers' podium at the March on Washington on August 28, 1963, to acknowledge the cheers of a grateful crowd,
Rustin was fifty-one years old, and had been working toward his dream for three
decades. He had endured jail, poverty, racism, physical violence, social os-

tracism, and political marginalization. He had served major radical and civil rights leaders, including King, as an adviser, strategist, and rhetoritician, but always from a position behind the scenes, a furtive necessity for the men who sought his talents but feared his "reputation."

But Rustin's shadow life ended on August 28, 1963. And this meant more than an elevated national profile. On that day, everything he had worked for, everything he had dreamed of, now seemed possible. The March on Washington for Jobs and Freedom had, as its title implied, fused demands for economic and racial justice. It sought the end of both the Southern Jim Crow system of legalized segregation and black voter disenfranchisement, which had been in place since the end of the nineteenth century, and a national government-sponsored jobs program, which was at the heart of Rustin's democratic socialist agenda.

In addition, the march had brought together civil rights leaders like King and labor leaders such as Walter Reuther of the United Auto Workers and Albert Shanker of New York's United Federation of Teachers, who also believed that the road to racial equality began with economic equality. The relationship between labor and race in America had long been uneasy. Employers had used African Americans as strikebreakers during labor disputes, at once crippling unions and inflaming racial animosities. For their part, American labor unions had been notoriously hostile to blacks. Segregated locals existed in the South for years; some craft unions barred blacks altogether. It was not until the 1930s and 1940s that the Congress of Industrial Organizations (CIO) began to incorporate large numbers of semi- and unskilled African Americans as part of its drive to organize heavy manufacturing sectors in steel, automobiles, rubber, and textiles. Even the CIO leadership's official stand against racial discrimination did not protect blacks from the hostility of white co-unionists, not to mention second-class treatment in matters relating to hiring, promotion, and work assignments. Rustin had spent the years preceding the March on Washington seeking to build an interracial labor movement, and now, on this greatest day of his life, with black and white labor leaders joining hands behind a platform that demanded both jobs and freedom, economic rights, and civil rights, his dream seemed close enough to touch.

But Rustin was to be bitterly disappointed. He spent the years between 1963 and his death in 1987 in the public eye, publishing articles and newspaper columns, appearing on television, consulting with major political leaders, and receiving honorary degrees. His new life outside the shadows, however, exacted a price. He learned over that last quarter century how difficult it would be to realize his American dream. New Leftists, Vietnam War protesters, and black separatists denounced him as an apologist for war, racism, and the "establishment" policies of the Democratic Party. His newfound access to the inner precincts of power never produced the results he envisioned. His hopes for a massive "Freedom Budget" to eradicate poverty in the United States were not fulfilled. His

Rustin standing in triumph at conclusion of March on Washington, August 28, 1963. Source: Corbis.

efforts to build an alliance between the labor and civil rights movements around a democratic socialist agenda came to naught. Rustin learned, in fact, that conflict between the two causes most dear to him, labor and civil rights, could force difficult, even impossible, choices. He also learned that the politics of racial identity in America was stronger than the politics of class, and the separatist impulse was stronger than that of integration. And as the nation's politics swung to the right in the late 1960s, 1970s, and 1980s, Rustin learned that Americans were almost as uncomfortable with economic integration as they were with integration by race. At his death in 1987, an outsider no more, his American dream remained beyond reach.

It is ironic that this most American of men, whose life embodied so many of his nation's values and aspirations, spent so much time on its margins. But for many years there seemed to be no place except the shadows for an ex-communist, a draft resister, and a homosexual who appeared to mock America's sense of itself. In time, Rustin emerged from those shadows and moved to "insider" status, a confidante of elected officials, labor leaders, and civil rights icons. But as he discovered, this new position came with its own burdens and perils. Few charges cut deeper than those of "sellout" and "establishment tool" leveled at an erstwhile revolutionary.

Yet his final twenty years were in many ways Rustin's most admirable. If the definition of a humanitarian is one who seeks to assist groups other than his own, then Rustin epitomized the term during those last years. He worked tirelessly on behalf of Soviet Jews who were imprisoned second-class citizens in their own country, while many of his former allies on the left remained silent. He traveled repeatedly to Southeast Asia to assist Vietnamese and Cambodian refugees, working to resettle them in the United States where they could begin new lives. He became a roving ambassador for international democracy, helping to monitor elections in El Salvador, Zimbabwe, Lebanon, and Haiti. At home, he continued to pursue his dream of a truly integrated American society, one that did not discriminate on the basis of skin color, or—just as important for Rustin—income. To the last, he fought for "people in trouble," no matter who they were.

Many of Rustin's American dreams did not come true. The United States did not turn toward socialism, pacifism, or racial and economic integration. But even as the structural transformations that Rustin sought remained elusive, America changed profoundly as a result of his life and work. Nonviolent direct action, which Rustin introduced as a philosophy and a strategy, established the modern civil rights movement as the most powerful moral force in twentieth-century American life. It destroyed a century-old edifice of white supremacy and racial segregation and made it possible for African Americans to attain and wield national political power. The thousands of elected black public officials in the United States today, including the mayors of Southern cities in which blacks could not even drink at "whites only" water fountains a generation ago, are the fruit of Rustin's belief in the power of representative democracy to make crooked paths straight. Rustin did not help elect the black mayors of Atlanta, Georgia, or Birmingham, Alabama, but he did help create an America in which they could be elected. Rustin's American dream made the United States a fairer, more inclusive, and more equal nation.

Rustin's defeats and victories, moreover, resonate beyond his own life, and even the life of his dreams. They illuminate the American experience of the twentieth century. His story is that of political, social, economic, and cultural life in the United States during that century. When Du Bois wrote in *The Souls of Black Folk* of the "double consciousness" of the American negro—his unique position at once inside and outside the American mainstream—he also noted the unique vantage point this position afforded African Americans.[3] Rustin's life offers these opportunities and more. A socialist in a capitalist nation, a black in a white nation, a pacifist in a militarized nation, and a homosexual in a homophobic nation, Rustin embodied the possibilities and limitations of an American dream that sought to change the basic structures of American society from both within and without. He exemplified the classic tension between the roles of "outsider" and "insider" with which advocates of systemic change in American social, political, and economic life have wrestled throughout the nation's history—between working outside established structures and institutions at the cost of power and influence and exchanging principles and ideals for access and inclusion. He may be the only American in history to have served both time in a federal penitentiary and as a part of the political network of a U.S. president.

Out of these tensions, which Rustin never fully resolved, comes a deeper understanding of the dilemmas facing American radicals as they searched for ways to affect the parameters of national life. They sometimes set the moral imperatives of civil rights, labor rights, pacifism, and socialism against each other, costing Rustin close friendships, political alliances, and the patronage of the powerful. As a result, his was a life of pain, defeat, and unrealized dreams. But it was also one that challenged the nation to honor the American dreams of Jefferson, Thoreau, Whitman, Lincoln, Du Bois, and Debs by fulfilling its unique promise of equality and freedom for all of its citizens. Rustin's life in shadow and sunlight spoke powerfully both to the past and the future of the American experience—as it was and yet can be.

Notes

1. W. E. B. Du Bois, *The Souls of Black Folk* (New York: Library of America, 1990), p. 9.
2. Du Bois, *The Souls of Black Folk*, p. 9.
3. Du Bois, *The Souls of Black Folk*, pp. 8–10.

CHAPTER ONE

~

Voice of Protest, 1912–1946

Bayard Rustin began his life on March 17, 1912, as far from the centers of power and influence in America as one could possibly be. He was the child of a teenage mother and a day laborer in the town of West Chester, Pennsylvania, just outside Philadelphia. Both his parents were black. They never married. Bayard knew his father only by reputation and had no relationship with him. His mother, Florence, was fifteen when he was born and in no position to raise him. She quickly ceded parental responsibilities to her own parents—Bayard's grandparents—and exited her son's life. He did not learn she was his mother until he was in grade school. By then, it scarcely mattered; he regarded his grandparents, Janifer and Julia Rustin, as his father and mother, and would continue to do so for the rest of his life.

West Chester, during Rustin's childhood and adolescence, was a diverse community that reflected the national immigration patterns of the previous decades. It was also absorbing African Americans from the South, its small portion of what became known as the First Great Migration. After the outbreak of World War I in 1914, Southern blacks poured north, fleeing poverty and racism. The war had stemmed the flow of white immigrants from Europe to the factories of the United States, creating opportunities for African Americans in Northern industry. The Great Migration changed the face of Northern cities. Before the war, with the vast majority of African Americans confined to the South, most Northern whites viewed race as a "Southern" problem. The movement of blacks northward after 1914 brought racial issues and tensions to their doorsteps.

These tensions also affected smaller cities like West Chester. Although Rustin's grandparents had roots in the area that preceded the Great Migration—Janifer had come to Pennsylvania from Maryland in the 1880s and Julia's family had resided there for generations—they and their grandchild were nonetheless affected by them. West Chester during the 1910s was a segregated town, in which certain public facilities, like theaters, were open to African Americans on a limited basis, and others—notably restaurants and downtown stores—did not cater to African Americans at all. Residential segregation was a given. The east end of town was the black section, and this is where Bayard grew up. Although white children lived nearby and friendships sometimes developed, it was always understood who belonged where. Rustin attended the all-black Gay Street Elementary School in the east end.

A rich home life provided some compensation for the slights and insults of the streets. Janifer was a kind, quiet man who gave young Bayard an example of dignity and strength. Although his work as a fraternal lodge steward did not offer the Rustin family prosperity, it did provide basic financial stability, and Bayard grew up free from the day-to-day insecurities of the truly impoverished. It was Julia Rustin, however, who influenced him the most. Like many in the area, Julia identified as a Quaker, and she represented Bayard's first exposure to a faith and philosophy that would become one of the driving forces of his life. Quakerism was deeply egalitarian. It emphasized the brotherhood of all human beings. It was especially hospitable to African Americans. Quakers had a long history of opposition to slavery. Many were active participants in the "Underground Railroad," a network of safe houses designed to spirit escaped slaves to freedom in the North and Canada, which included a number of Quaker-owned homes in West Chester itself. It was logical, then, for the religion to appeal to Julia. If any branch of Christianity could be associated with the cause of civil rights during Bayard's youth, it was Quakerism.

Julia taught her grandson to take a stand against racial injustice, advice he never forgot. One of the first members of the fledgling National Association for the Advancement of Colored People (NAACP), she entertained W. E. B. Du Bois and other civil rights leaders of the day in her home. Thanks to Julia, Bayard always knew who he was. She also imbued him with an ethos of compassion and empathy for other human beings, whomever they were. This derived in part from her Quaker heritage, as well as her experiences as an African American in the late nineteenth and early twentieth centuries.

But there was in addition a more generalized humanitarian impulse, a concern for the weak and the persecuted regardless of skin color. Julia stood out in a racially and ethnically divided community for her willingness to welcome all children into her home. She trained Bayard to treat everyone equally—with compassion, understanding, and empathy. She would send food to the homes of Bayard's white friends when illness struck. She once upbraided her grandson for ridiculing a local man known to be an alcoholic. All human beings, she told him, were children of God.[1] It is, of course, impossible to link Rustin's later humanitarianism, his advocacy for "people in trouble," to any one source. But the genesis of his persona as a civil rights leader who viewed "equality" in universal terms and who refused to conflate "justice" with the claims of African Americans alone, may well have come from Julia, who remained a source of advice and support until her death in 1957.

Rustin's mind was extraordinary in its breadth and power. Although he benefited from the guidance of sympathetic teachers and a home atmosphere in which learning was prized, his was largely a self-generated intellect. He was well versed in the Bible, American history, and classical literature and music. By the time he entered West Chester High School in 1928, he had burnished his scholarly reputation by developing a formal, British-sounding manner of speaking, a linguistic tic that stayed with him for the rest of his life. But this was incidental to his success in high school. One of the relatively few blacks in the school, Rustin was its unquestioned star. He played tackle on a championship football

Rustin at the time of his high school graduation, 1932.
Source: Estate of Bayard Rustin.

team and helped set a record for the mile relay in track. Possessing a beautiful singing voice, he won admirers for his renditions of opera arias. He was an accomplished actor, orator, and writer. He also excelled academically and graduated with high honors. Showered with accolades at graduation, he spoke to and sang before his graduating class, the epitome of the "big man on campus."

It was, however, 1932, in the depths of the Great Depression, a terrible time for a white high school graduate to be making his way in the world, never mind a black one. There were few established patterns of advancement for talented African American youths in the United States of the 1930s, but there did exist a network of colleges founded during the nineteenth century that were dedicated to the education and "uplift" of promising black students. They provided an outlet for these students, albeit a racially circumscribed one. Wilberforce University, near Xenia, Ohio, was such an institution. Wilberforce had been established before the Civil War as the nation's first all-black institution of higher learning. It had developed a fine reputation in music, a good fit for Rustin's interests. Through a family friend who had just become the school's president, Rustin was awarded a scholarship to Wilberforce. He arrived there in September 1932, and remained there for two years. As in high school, he excelled in voice, starring in the college's chorus, which traveled the country giving performances. But Rustin's deepening Quaker convictions ran afoul of Wilberforce's Reserve Officers' Training Corps (ROTC) policy, which imposed a program of military instruction on all male students. Wilberforce was not the school for someone with Rustin's independence and curiosity. In 1934 he dropped out and returned to West Chester and his grandparents.

One of the unstated reasons for Rustin's departure from Wilberforce was the blossoming of his homosexuality, which occurred during his time there. His first homosexual encounter had come in his early teenage years, with an older man living at the home of his mother. Thereafter, his impulses grew stronger, until he was compelled to acknowledge them, both to himself and to a small group of close friends. They in turn did their best to shield him from the humiliations and dangers faced by those who transgressed the sexual boundaries of the time. There was no accepted social role for a homosexual in the America of Rustin's young manhood, no public space in which he could "be." Harassed by police, blackmailed, and shaken down by law enforcement officials, gays learned to make themselves invisible to the "straight" world. They constructed an alternative society beneath the surface of the dominant sexual culture, usually in large cities that offered a veil of anonymity. There, homosexuals could establish personal connections indirectly and subtly, in parks, clubs, bars, and out-of-the-way neighborhoods.

As Rustin grew into his sexuality, he began to find lovers in this manner. Although he was not "closeted" in the traditional sense of conducting liaisons in private while feigning heterosexuality, neither did he make his sexual choices a public issue during this period of his life. At a time when politics was starting to inform much of his existence, he viewed his homosexuality as a personal matter. Not until his last decade would this change. As he prepared to resume his college career near West Chester at Cheyney State Teachers' College in September 1934, his homosexuality—what his friends sometimes condescendingly referred to as "Bayard's problem"—remained a potentially dangerous part of his private life.

Rustin's years at Cheyney State were much more challenging and productive than his disappointing tenure at Wilberforce, although he once again left without a degree. Although both Cheyney and Wilberforce were "historically black" colleges, the Pennsylvania school opened more broadly to the wider world. It offered an opportunity for a liberal arts education, as opposed to Wilberforce's vocational orientation. Befitting an institution established by Quakers, ethical and moral questions, including those relating to war and peace, dominated Cheyney's discourse. Its atmosphere matched Rustin's own intellectual aspirations. As he had in the past, he made a name musically, singing in the school chorus, often as a well-received soloist. But he also studied philosophy and threw himself into the debates over war and peace that had turned the campus into a political cauldron during this time.

Between 1934 and 1937, the years Rustin attended Cheyney, the rise of aggressive totalitarianism in Europe had forced students at the school to confront both the broad question of America's world role and the more immediate issue of whether to take up arms in the event of conflict. The rabidly nationalistic and anti-Semitic Adolf Hitler, having come to power in 1933, was rapidly remilitarizing Germany, repudiating the Treaty of Versailles that had ended World War I, withdrawing from the League of Nations and threatening the security of democracies across Europe. Benito Mussolini, the fascist dictator of Italy, had also launched a campaign of rearmament and expansionism, defying the League of Nations by seizing Ethiopia in 1936. Both men offered military aid to General Francisco Franco, whose 1936 revolt against the democratically elected government of Spain had launched a bloody civil war. On the left, Joseph Stalin's Soviet regime was in the process of purging millions of "counterrevolutionaries" and "Western spies" in a bloodbath of monumental proportions. The world during Rustin's years at Cheyney was clearly a dangerous place. But what to do about it? In 1936 he formally joined the Society of Friends and declared himself a Quaker. Rustin decided to take a stand against totalitarian military aggression by opposing war itself, and pacifism would henceforth be one of the defining impulses of his life.

By the next year, he was a leading antiwar spokesman on campus and made his first foray into pacifist activism. He participated in the Institute of International

Relations, a program organized by the American Friends Service Committee (AFSC), a Quaker-sponsored outreach group. The institute attracted students and faculty from a national array of colleges and universities. The delegates decried the worldwide drift toward war and—significantly for Rustin's future as a socialist—linked it to the class inequities of unregulated capitalism. During the summer of 1937, he served in the AFSC's Peace Brigade, in which students traveled to various locations as grassroots pacifist organizers. Rustin spent that summer in Auburn, New York, where he taught, wrote, spoke, and preached on behalf of peace. Coming only two decades after World War I, a murderous and ultimately disillusioning experience for many Americans, his message was received with some degree of sympathy; American isolationist sentiment in 1937 was strong, especially outside urban areas.

But there was more to Rustin's brand of pacifism than the mere rejection of violence. It also featured a commitment to social justice that was inseparable from the antiwar impulse. Peace as an end in itself was not enough. Only if yoked to a broader vision of national equality could the peace movement have any lasting meaning. Rustin's pacifism was developing into an ambitious, transformative vision that employed nonviolence both on its own terms and as a means to end racial discrimination and equalize economic opportunity in the United States. In his hands, this vision would become "nonviolent direct action," the strategy and philosophy that changed American race relations in the 1950s and 1960s. During the summer of 1937, Rustin's yearnings—for peace, for racial equality, for economic justice—were forming into an American dream that was uniquely his own.

In the fall of 1937 Rustin left Cheyney State and moved to New York City. On one level, this change was understandable. New York City was America's open city. It was where the nation's radical political and cultural currents converged, a logical destination for a young man with Rustin's dreams. But he dropped out of Cheyney at the beginning of what would have been his senior year, an especially puzzling decision for someone whose time at the school had been rewarding and successful. It is possible that his homosexuality may have been responsible for his premature exit. Leslie Hill, the college's president, was a strict moralist, and he could have heard of one of Rustin's liaisons with a white boy in West Chester. In any event, it was probably time for him to go. If a black homosexual could be himself anywhere, it was in New York.

Rustin arrived in the city in the fall of 1937. Henceforth it would be his home, the place to which he would always return. New York was a city of many cultures and subcultures, and Rustin took advantage of what it offered. Harlem was his first stop. He lived briefly with his Aunt Bessie, a teacher, in the St. Nicholas Avenue area known as Sugar Hill—so named for its concentration of black professionals and businessmen—before finding his own apartment in the neighborhood. He supported himself by teaching English to immigrants at a local high school, a job he obtained through the New Deal's Works Progress Administration (WPA).

The WPA, one of the signature programs of the presidency of Franklin D. Roosevelt (1882–1945), provided government-sponsored work to the unemployed during the Great Depression. It provided Rustin with an example of the national state as employer of last resort and economic safety net. Wherever he looked during his early years in New York, Rustin could see the results of the government's largesse. It helped people in trouble. The 1930s and 1940s marked the height of federal, state, and local governments' involvement in the lives of New York City's citizens. Activist Mayor Fiorello La Guardia (1882–1947) had established municipal government as a benign, protective force in daily life. It gave jobs to the unemployed and welfare assistance to the poor. It utilized federal funding to construct an impressive infrastructure of bridges, tunnels, highways, and parks that continue to serve as the city's backbone today. The State of New York was a pioneer in generous social services, a model for the New Deal itself. And through the National Labor Relations Act of 1935, the Social Security Act of the same year, and an array of other legislative enactments and programs, including the WPA, Franklin D. Roosevelt forged the federal government into a powerful champion of the "forgotten American."

These examples of federal, state, and local government-sponsored good works affected Rustin deeply. They led him to a lifelong faith in the power of government to improve lives, and even save them. An individualist in his personal behavior, Rustin believed that citizens were responsible for one another, and that this ethic of mutual obligation should govern political and economic life in the United States. This put him in conflict with a well-established American ethos of competition and acquisitiveness. For good or ill, the Protestant Ethic—the idea that material success is a sign of God's favor, thus justifying capitalism as an economic system—has had a profound impact on American society. Rustin spent much of his career swimming against its strong cultural tide. Although he often seemed to occupy a position outside the national mainstream on economic issues, Rustin's understanding of the inequities of class in American society enabled him to influence that mainstream even as an outsider. One need not be a socialist or communist to believe in the efficacy of government action on behalf of the disadvantaged, and Rustin eventually became a powerful advocate for "big government" liberalism, propelling it toward his dream of economic security for every American.

In New York, Rustin moved between black and white cultures, between Harlem and Greenwich Village. He joined an interracial, sexually diverse group of young leftists whose liberated sensibilities meshed with his. Although gay life in New York was not completely open, it was freer than in any other American city. Authorities would prosecute overt homosexual activity, but would not reach into private lives or the home to do so. This afforded gays an informal "space," albeit a restricted one, for self-expression. Rustin could thus socialize with other gay men in bars, clubs, restaurants, theaters, and residences.

The city's homosexual subculture flowed into its artistic world. Here too, Rustin quickly fit in. His musical talents earned him a small role on Broadway in a play headlined by stage legend—and legendary political radical—Paul Robeson. Soon afterward, Rustin joined Josh White and the Carolinians, a black folk group with leftist political leanings. White, like Robeson, had ties to the American Communist Party. The Carolinians played regularly at Café Society, a Greenwich Village nightclub that fused music and radical politics. Rustin's performing life merged into his political world, exposing him to men and women engaged in the struggle for class and racial justice in America. This world was interracial, in which the customary barriers between blacks and whites were lowered, permitting levels of intimacy unheard of in the rest of the country. Rustin's political, racial, and sexual environments thus connected, creating an atmosphere as close to Walt Whitman's ideal of communal self-expression as at any previous time in the nation's history. Out of it grew the three great dreams of Rustin's life: civil rights, economic justice, and pacifism.

Each of these alone, of course, comprises the work of a lifetime, and it is a testament to the breadth of Rustin's vision that he sought to embrace them all. But his reach would exceed his grasp. Over the course of his long career as an activist, his dreams often conflicted. One would make demands upon him that he could only fulfill at the expense of the others. The moral weight of each often made compromises between them almost impossible, and he would be forced into wrenching choices amid personal accusations and charges of betrayal. Rustin was one of the rare Americans in whom powerful impulses toward racial equality, labor rights, and peace existed simultaneously. His efforts to reconcile them, and to square the circle of American radical politics, would result in professional disappointment and personal heartbreak.

Rustin's early New York years offered the first examples of this unresolved dilemma. Rustin joined the Young Communist League, the youth wing of the Communist Party of the United States (CPUSA) soon after moving to the city. The 1930s marked the high point of the party's relationship with the nation's African American population. No other left-wing entity supported civil rights causes with such dedication and fervor. The Communists believed that African Americans were the key ingredients in the Marxist revolution they planned for the United States. If blacks could be united with working-class whites, their alliance would smash capitalism. The Communist International (Comintern), through which the Soviet Union sought to export Marxism to foreign countries, directed American Communists to concentrate their energy on bringing blacks into the party fold. The CPUSA established its civil rights reputation in 1931 when it launched a spirited defense of the "Scottsboro Boys," a group of black Alabama youths wrongfully convicted of raping two white women. It was this aspect of occupying the front lines in the fight for racial justice that attracted Rustin to the Communists. He served the party as a youth organizer for the State of New York and on a committee to integrate the armed services.

The Communist orbit was particularly attractive to Rustin between 1939 and 1941, the years of the Hitler-Stalin pact. In August 1939 the Soviet Union entered into an alliance of convenience with its ideological and geopolitical archenemy, Nazi Germany, permitting the latter to invade Poland. World War II began days afterward. The CPUSA, a slavish follower of the Soviet "party line," proclaimed its opposition to America's involvement in the war. Many members left in disillusionment over the party's betrayal of its principles. For years, Soviet leaders had portrayed the Nazi regime as the essence of evil. Now they were allies. Rustin, however, stayed in the CPUSA. Its new antiwar position dovetailed perfectly with his pacifism. Between 1939 and 1941, in fact, the party provided a vehicle for all three of his causes—peace, civil rights, and Marxism. But in the wake of Hitler's June 1941 attack on the Soviet Union, the CPUSA executed a 180-degree turn and embraced all-out interventionism. As always, the survival of the USSR was the party's top priority. Accordingly, it instructed its members to desist from all activities that would interfere with America's entry into and prosecution of the war. After the Japanese attack on Pearl Harbor on December 7, 1941, brought the United States into World War II, the CPUSA proscribed civil rights agitation and cut ties to the nation's peace movement.

Rustin was now forced to choose between his commitments to pacifism and racial justice. He had continued his involvement with the AFSC after moving to New York, becoming active in its support programs for draft resisters. Rustin's allegiance to pacifism was growing during these years to embrace a moral absolutism that made him willing to accept prison rather than submit to a government that sponsored war, even a war to defeat Nazism. At the same time, he was becoming increasingly active in civil rights causes. Through the CPUSA, he had become active in the Committee Against Discrimination in the Armed Forces, which worked to integrate the racially segregated American military. In addition, Rustin confronted the issue of employment bias in New York's black neighborhoods. African Americans had long resented the refusal of many white-owned Harlem businesses to hire them, despite constituting the bulk of their customer base. In the late 1930s, Adam Clayton Powell, a local minister and future congressman, organized a "Don't Buy Where You Can't Work" boycott of discriminatory Harlem retailers, in which Rustin played an active role.

The campaign's successful use of economic pressure to achieve its goals—virtually all Harlem businesses adopted integrated hiring practices—made a profound impression on Rustin. He saw firsthand the power of mass protest to influence white institutions and effectuate racial change. He also saw, however, that mass power alone was not enough. Protest, he concluded, must be nonviolent, interracial (left-wing and liberal whites, including many CPUSA members, had assisted the boycott), and fixed on an opponent's weakness—in this case the white businessman's need for black patronage. The "Don't Buy Where You Can't Work" campaign taught Rustin that unfocused, diffuse protest, even when motivated by high moral principles, did not produce systemic change. The March on Washington Movement, with which he became involved in 1941, reinforced this lesson on a national scale.

The movement had been organized by the leading African American labor leader of his time, A. Philip Randolph (1889–1979). During the 1920s and 1930s, Randolph had founded and built the Brotherhood of Sleeping Car Porters, the most powerful black union in the United States. He did so against daunting odds, defeating both Jim Crow and the barons of the railroad industry with an appeal to his members as both workers and African Americans. This melding of labor and civil rights, employed so successfully during the struggle to organize the sleeping car porters, became Randolph's philosophical template for the rest of his career.

Randolph was a democratic socialist who believed that the nation's racial inequities were inseparable from those relating to material conditions, and that racism could not be understood outside the context of class injustice. He thus viewed African Americans as workers whose potential cross-racial alliances with their white counterparts could alter the patterns of social and economic life in the United States. In this sense, Randolph and Rustin were traveling the same road even before they met, and it was almost inevitable that their paths would eventually cross. Rustin and Randolph were casual acquaintances when Randolph announced a march on the nation's capital, scheduled for July 1941, to demand an end to racial discrimination in defense-related industries. It would be the first mass march of African Americans on Washington, D.C., in the nation's history.

Randolph called on Rustin to be the youth organizer for the march. Thus began a professional and personal association that would last for the rest of their lives. Despite the quarter-century difference in their ages, the two men had much in common. Both held to an American dream that fused racial and economic egalitarianism. Both believed in the power of an interracial alliance of the working class and poor to realize that dream. Both had an almost mystical belief in the labor movement as an instrument of social justice. Moreover, each had a deep need for the other: the childless Randolph for a son, and the abandoned Rustin for a father figure. Randolph became Rustin's mentor, confessor, and champion for most of the next four decades.

Randolph's planned march deeply concerned President Roosevelt. Desperate to mobilize the nation for a war that by early 1941 loomed ominously, he viewed the march as a distraction at best, and at worst, a major blow to the preparedness effort. He pressured Randolph to call it off, to no avail. Finally, with no other alternative, Roosevelt issued Executive Order 8802 on June 25, 1941, banning discrimination in defense industry hiring and establishing a Fair Employment Practice Committee to monitor compliance. With his major objective achieved, Randolph canceled the march. Rustin, who had made recruiting trips through the Northeast and Midwest on behalf of the youth division, objected. He argued that an aroused black community needed to be heard, notwithstanding Roosevelt's order, and that the march would be a powerful symbolic expression of its discontent. But the more pragmatic Randolph understood that while symbols were gratifying, substance was real. He had achieved his main goal without risking embarrassment, since attendance at an actual march might prove disappointing. Substance trumped symbolism—this was the first of many lessons Rustin would learn from Randolph. In time he came to understand that practical, tangible gains were preferable to empty emotional victories.

Although Randolph's decision to call off the march disappointed Rustin, he coupled it with one more to his protégé's liking. Randolph announced the formation of the March on Washington Movement to continue the fight for civil rights through nonviolence, allowing Rustin to maintain his connection with him. Randolph also introduced Rustin to a man who would become his other great influence, the Christian pacifist A. J. Muste. Trained as a Dutch Reformed minister, Muste (1885–1967) was a veteran white social and political activist. During the 1920s and 1930s he had been a radical labor leader who organized unskilled industrial workers on an interracial basis. He had also been a supporter of the anti-Stalinist Marxist ideologue Leon Trotsky, and, by 1940, was a self-styled Christian revolutionary whose weapon of choice was nonviolent direct action. That year Muste assumed the leadership of the Fellowship of Reconciliation (FOR), a pacifist group that had been founded in England during World War I and grew in the United States as a vehicle of antiwar protest. Primarily white and upper class in membership, it had been a comparatively staid organization when Muste assumed its leadership, committed to a narrowly gauged pacifism that stood for little more than a generalized opposition to war.

Muste immediately set out to broaden FOR's goals and vision. The "new" FOR would feature a militant Christianity that sought not merely the abolition of war, but a social, political, and economic revolution in American life. Nonviolent direct action would be its instrument. Muste's version of the doctrine combined the civil disobedience philosophy of Henry David Thoreau, the religious sensibility of the Quakers, and the radical insurgency of the leader of India's independence movement, Mahatma Gandhi. By 1940 Gandhi's mass protest strategies were turning the tide in the struggle against British colonialism and attracting worldwide attention. Muste saw in them the seeds of a new American nation, free from the scourges of racism, poverty, and war.

Nonviolent direct action held enormous transformative potential. It reversed the usual dynamics of power by using the weight of the strong to impart strength to the weak. Practitioners of nonviolent direct action deliberately violated unjust laws and social practices in order to dramatize their evil effects to the broader public. Once men and women of goodwill understood the magnitude of these injustices, they would themselves act to end them. In the meantime, the nonviolent protesters would willingly accept the consequences of their transgressions. They would endure the harshest punishments with equanimity, in the spirit of love and forgiveness. They would strike out at oppression, but not at the oppressor. Their sacrifices would eventually move the consciences of those who persecuted them, as well as the wider circle of concerned observers. The nation as a whole would unite to drive out evil and build a society based on Christian virtue, one rooted in love for one's fellows. In the process, the unjust laws, practices, and institutions dramatized through nonviolence would fall before its moral imperatives.

But nonviolent direct action was more than a tactic to effect change. It was also a way of life, a means to uplift the soul. When nonviolent protesters embraced suffering and loved even their oppressors, they brought themselves closer to God. It was a philosophy that did as much for those who lived it as those they sought to help. In Muste's hands, then, nonviolent direct action would purify both its practitioner and its object. He expected denial and sacrifice from his followers. Muste had no patience for self-promotion. His only interests lay in his causes, and in 1941, as war raged in Europe, and economic and racial inequalities persisted in the United States, these included peace, the plight of the poor and working class, and civil rights. Muste's newly reconfigured FOR was the perfect place for Bayard Rustin to be.

Rustin was still a Communist in June 1941. But that month's invasion of the Soviet Union by Nazi Germany pushed him away from the CPUSA and toward Muste and Randolph. Rustin had been working for the desegregation of the U.S. military under the Communist Party auspices, but its postinvasion directive to cease all civil rights–related activities, as well as its newly minted rejection of pacifism, had placed him in an impossible position. When party leaders demanded that he leave the Committee Against Discrimination in the Armed Forces and support what they now viewed as a "good war," Rustin refused and quit the CPUSA. He became a staunch anti-Communist for the rest of his life. In September 1941, he joined FOR as youth secretary.

FOR employees during the 1940s needed the commitment, forbearance, and self-control of saints. Rustin was paid a pittance, assigned a crushing work schedule that required him to be on the road for weeks at a time, and asked to promote a message that, with the nation's entry into World War II in December 1941, was hardly calculated to resonate with the American public. Nonetheless, Rustin loved FOR. It offered a community of the like-minded, a tight-knit group of young idealists hoping to use nonviolence to change America and the world. Unlike the Communist Party, FOR did not require Rustin to choose between civil rights, economic justice, and peace: it embraced all three. He plunged into his work in the field and at FOR headquarters, near Columbia University in Upper Manhattan, with a sense of grand possibility.

Rustin traveled the country, organizing local FOR chapters, speaking at churches and schools, and offering support to conscientious objectors. Wherever he went, he was an unforgettable presence. Tall, leanly muscular, impeccably attired, Rustin would make the case for peace in compelling, often inspiring, language. Sometimes he would sing, employing the musical talents cultivated in his youth and early days in New York. Spirituals were his forte. His eloquence and musicality often moved his audiences to tears. As he traveled, Rustin began

Rustin and FOR activists protest imprisonment of war protesters during World War II. Source: Estate of Bayard Rustin.

to focus on racial issues as much as on peace. At FOR, he had begun working with James Farmer, a young African American pacifist and recent graduate of Howard University Divinity School. Like Rustin, Farmer had a deep interest in racial justice and a desire to employ nonviolence to achieve it. The two men convinced Muste to have FOR sponsor a new, secular organization that would devote itself to this cause. In April 1942 the Congress of Racial Equality (CORE) came into being as FOR's secular civil rights arm. CORE permitted Rustin to return to his roots on college campuses, since it was primarily an organization of the young. It also allowed him to sidestep a relatively unpalatable message—since in the face of a popular war, pacifism was a difficult "sell"—and instead focus on the use of nonviolence for racial equity.

Rustin also remained active in Randolph's March on Washington Movement and was instrumental in its adoption of nonviolent direct action as an official strategy in July 1943. Randolph asked for permission to use Rustin as a point man in his effort to desegregate the U.S. military, ironically the same task that Rustin had undertaken for the CPUSA before the Nazi invasion of the Soviet Union. By 1943 Rustin was dividing his time between FOR, CORE, and the March on Washington Movement, articulating a message that blended his passions for civil rights, peace, and socialism. He was able to reach a diverse group of Americans, including middle-class, church-based whites through FOR; students and activist blacks through CORE; and the broader African American community through the March on Washington Movement.

Rustin's dream of knitting these constituencies along with working-class whites into a collective force for racial and economic equality in the United States began to mature here. He believed that finding common denominators among groups with partially overlapping agendas held the key to realizing the changes in American society that he imagined. In this sense, Rustin was both a dreamer and a pragmatist, committed to an ideal but realistic about what was necessary to achieve it. This quality also distinguished him among American radicals. Most who view the world in moral terms have difficulty accepting more self-interested perspectives. Rustin's willingness to accommodate other agendas in the service of a larger cause gave him a breadth and scope that more conventional radicals lacked. It was also making him a name. By 1943 it seemed that everyone on the American left knew Bayard Rustin.

Rustin's personal life was blossoming as well. In 1943 he met Davis Platt, a twenty-year-old white student, and began his first committed homosexual relationship. Platt enrolled at Columbia University to be closer to Rustin's FOR workplace, and the two became lovers, to the dismay of Muste. Straitlaced in matters of personal behavior, he sought to dissuade them. FOR, after all, was a religious organization, and even the most radical and racially egalitarian Christian activists during the 1940s had difficulty accepting homosexuality. Muste viewed Rustin's sexual behavior as a potential embarrassment to the organiza-tion. His protégé's sexuality would be an ongoing source of tension between the two men over the course of the next decade.

In late 1943 the sword that had been hanging over Rustin's personal and pro-fessional life dropped. From the moment America entered World War II, Rustin had been expecting a draft call. As a pacifist and FOR staffer, he could easily have qualified for a deferment. The federal government offered conscientious objectors the option of "civilian public service," consisting of work at a series of labor camps scattered around the country. But to a committed activist like Rustin, this smacked of an unholy bargain with injustice, precisely what mem-bers of FOR were taught to reject. The camps to which the objectors were sent were isolated and offered little in the way of meaningful work. They amounted to holding pens designed to keep war protesters out of circulation. Rustin de-cided to accept prison instead. There, he could put his ideas about nonviolent resistance into action, challenging both the war and the inequities of the penal system through a program of deliberate disobedience. He notified his New York draft board that he would not participate in any registration procedure, and pled guilty to draft evasion in February 1944. He was sentenced to three years in a federal penitentiary.

Rustin's choice was especially risky—and courageous—in the light of his per-sonal circumstances and political background. His stated aim was to disrupt a system that was authoritarian by definition, immediately marking him as a "troublemaker." He was a "draft dodger" in the midst of America's most popular war. He was an African American. He was a civil rights crusader. And, of course, he was moving into an atmosphere fraught with danger for homosexu-als, in which he would be regarded as a "deviant" by guards and inmates alike. Rustin was determined, nonetheless, to use his prison experience to dramatize the causes of racial justice, peace, and nonviolence. In a precursor of what would become a commonplace form of protest during the 1960s, he would place his body on the wheels of the federal prison machine in an effort to disrupt its operation. And he would accept the punishments, physical and otherwise, that his actions elicited. Bureau of Prisons officials seemed eager to oblige him. Rustin was assigned to the penitentiary at Ashland, Kentucky, where he arrived in March 1944.

Ashland was located on the Ohio River, just across from the North, and it was rural, isolated, and very much a "Southern" place. Its inmate population in-cluded a small cohort of conscientious objectors, but a much larger number of "hard cases" from the white South, whose racial attitudes were fixed, hostile, and often expressed violently. At a time when the nation needed every soldier it could muster, the mere fact that these men were in prison at all testified to their incorrigibility. The prison guards were themselves only a few steps away from the wrong side of the law. Into this environment came a defiant Rustin, refusing to acknowledge the legitimacy of the prison system and intent on testing it at every turn.

It did not take him long to become notorious at Ashland for his deliberate flouting of rules that he considered unjust, especially those separating the races. The facility housed black and white prisoners in segregated areas. Rustin made it his goal to break down the barriers between the two through nonviolent action. He deliberately violated the spatial divisions of the prison, visiting the white cell areas whenever the mood struck him. Eventually the warden, while continuing to officially support segregation at Ashland, allowed the gate separating the races to be left unlocked in Rustin's section. Rustin took advantage of this informal relaxation of the rules to visit white war resisters on their side of the prison. One such visit aroused the wrath of a white Southern inmate, who set upon Rustin with a long stick and beat him viciously. Rustin remained physically passive during the attack, while explaining the principles of nonviolent social change to his enraged assailant.

On the surface, this would appear to be an incongruous, even tragicomic scene. A white man, screaming racial epithets, clubs a black man, who attempts to conduct an impromptu seminar on the teachings of, among others, Mahatma Gandhi. But Rustin's reaction was entirely consistent with his principles. FOR and CORE activists viewed violence as an opportunity to show both their personal commitment to the cause of nonviolent social change and their willingness to extend the spirit of brotherhood even to their oppressors. And so Rustin allowed himself to be struck repeatedly by a furious white man, offering no defense, save an explanation of nonviolence and an expression of empathy with his attacker. The white inmate's response spoke to the power of Rustin's words and demeanor. Robbed of the moral initiative, he finally sank back in exhaustion and frustration. He had broken Rustin's wrist, but he was clearly the loser in their encounter. Rustin had turned his tormentor's physical strength against him.

Rustin confronted a system of racial segregation at Ashland that bent but would not break. He managed to extract small compromises from the prison authorities, including permission to teach reading and civics to white inmates and the integration of church services. But overall progress was slow. The prison system was designed to be institutionally rigid, and the concept of an inmate as an agent of social change was foreign to administrators. To them, Rustin was an enigma and a threat. There would, of course, always be troublemakers in a penitentiary, but very few with Rustin's combination of principle and courage.

Ashland's warden, Robert Hagerman, was in constant contact with the Bureau of Prisons in Washington, requesting guidance in dealing with this apparently unmanageable inmate. There was little in the way of concrete advice his superiors could offer. But Rustin's sexual proclivities gave authorities the opportunity to reassert themselves. In September 1944 a prison disciplinary board found Rustin guilty of engaging in homosexual acts with another prisoner and placed him in isolation. Rustin denied all charges, but was convicted by eyewitness testimony. Muste was furious when he heard of the incident. He chastised Rustin for allowing his passions to jeopardize his campaign to desegregate Ashland. Rustin broke down and apologized, promising to reevaluate his sexual persona so as to comport with his Christian activism. Implicit in this promise was the assumption that homosexuality was inherently sinful and that it diminished his moral example. It would not be until late in life that Rustin was able to reconcile his sexuality and his politics. In 1944, however, he did not view sexual expression as a form of political expression; certainly his mentor never did so. Although Rustin's promise to "reform" brought him back into Muste's good graces, the issue of homosexuality eventually led to Rustin's forced departure from FOR.

Exasperated by his ongoing resistance and agitation, Warden Hagerman succeeded in having Rustin transferred to Lewisburg Federal Prison in August 1945, just as the war he had opposed so vigorously was coming to an end. Lewisburg, in central Pennsylvania, was designed for prisoners serving long sentences and was in many instances their last stop. Federal officials counted on this forbidding place to bring Rustin under control. But he continued to resist, now lashing out at all aspects of prison life. A hunger strike to protest segregated facilities landed Rustin in the hospital, where Muste visited him in March 1946. The older man pleaded with his disciple to moderate his behavior in order to secure an early release. Peace activists faced new challenges in a post-war, Cold War era. There were also new possibilities for racial justice in a nation that had just fought a war against bigotry and intolerance. In these circumstances, Rustin was more valuable as a free man than at Lewisburg. What walls, guards, and racist inmates could not do, Muste accomplished. Rustin began adhering to basic prison regimens and accumulating good behavior time. In June 1946 Lewisburg authorities, presumably with much relief, set him free.

Note

1. Daniel Levine, *Bayard Rustin and the Civil Rights Movement* (New Brunswick, NJ: Rutgers University Press, 2000), p. 10.

CHAPTER TWO

~

Toward Peace and Racial Justice, 1946–1963

Rustin rejoined the FOR staff immediately upon his release from prison in 1946. CORE offered him the chance to plunge into civil rights work, and a Supreme Court decision presented an unexpected opportunity to attack Jim Crow. In *Morgan v. Virginia*, issued as Rustin was leaving Lewisburg in June 1946, the Court invalidated all forms of discrimination in travel between states, including bus lines. But the opinion would have little or no effect on the South's segregated transportation practices unless outside forces came to bear. The federal government would not act. Although the administration of newly inaugurated President Harry S. Truman had established a special civil rights commission at the end of 1946, it was inconceivable that he would use federal power to alter the patterns of everyday life in the South. Into this political and moral vacuum stepped CORE. The issue of integrated public transportation fit its agenda perfectly. CORE could employ nonviolent direct action under relatively advantageous circumstances, in this instance seeking to enforce a just court ruling rather than defy an unjust one. Rustin and his CORE colleagues jumped at the opportunity to enforce what was now the law of the land by putting their bodies on the line.

Their project would be called the Journey of Reconciliation. As planned by Rustin and CORE executive secretary George Houser, it would send interracial pairs on buses through Virginia, North Carolina, Tennessee, and Kentucky to challenge segregation and enforce the *Morgan* decision. Rustin and Houser recruited a team of fourteen men, divided equally by race, to ride south with them. They all came from the radical wings of the pacifist and civil rights movements. Rustin tried to interest the mainstream press in the Journey, but only two black newspapers provided coverage, an indication of CORE's low profile in the national media at the time. The protesters left Washington, D.C., on April 9, 1947, bound for Richmond, Virginia. An interracial pair rode in both the white front and the black rear sections of the buses, in order to fully challenge the seating arrangements.

At first the rides went comparatively smoothly. Some drivers grumbled as the buses went through Virginia, but there were no arrests, and some white passengers even voiced support for the group. But North Carolina was another matter. A white rider was arrested on the way into Raleigh. Rustin himself was placed under arrest in Durham. But the most trouble occurred in, of all places, Chapel Hill, the home of the University of North Carolina and a town with a reputation for racial tolerance. There, six riders, including Rustin, boarded a bus, with an interracial pair sitting in both the white and black sections. The driver had the pair in front arrested, whereupon Rustin, who had been in the back, moved forward with his white partner. They too were arrested. After the four posted bail and were released, they were taken to the home of Charles Jones, a white minister and FOR member, where the rest of the riders had gathered. But a group of white taxi drivers who had observed the arrests at the Chapel Hill bus terminal from their adjacent stand caravanned to the Jones house and put it under siege. Throwing rocks through the windows, they threatened to burn it down. Only the arrival of the police, as well as a contingent of white Univer-

Rustin about to begin the Journey of Reconciliation with CORE members, Washington, D.C., April 9, 1947. Source: Estate of Bayard Rustin.

sity of North Carolina students, prevented the house from being overrun. The riders fled in a fleet of cars to Greensboro. Rustin would later serve twenty-two days on a North Carolina chain gang for his attempt to integrate the Chapel Hill bus. None of the white attackers were arrested.

The Journey continued through North Carolina and into Tennessee and Kentucky. Along the way Rustin held meetings to explain the group's philosophy and state the case for the desegregation of public facilities in the South. As was so often the case, the force of his mind, words, and personality was such that few audiences ever forgot him. But Rustin was largely preaching to the converted, the small number of Southern racial liberals. The mass constituency necessary to change the region's racial landscape eluded him, and the Journey of Reconciliation concluded with Southern buses still divided by race. But the Journey was seminal, not so much on its own terms but as a precursor of the future. In 1961 CORE members would once again ride south on interstate buses in order to desegregate them, in what came to be known as the Freedom Rides. The civil rights movement was in full swing by then, and unlike the Journey of Reconciliation, the Freedom Rides generated national publicity and achieved success. But the latter-day CORE activists had the advantage of working from a model of interracial nonviolent protest that Rustin and his fellows had pioneered. They walked a path already cleared by others. In this sense, the 1947 Journey of Reconciliation was the original Freedom Ride, and the real beginning of the modern civil rights movement.

Later in 1947 Rustin was reunited with Randolph, who had launched a campaign to desegregate the U.S. military. The timing was advantageous. As the Cold War with the Soviet Union heated up, President Truman faced a pressing need for manpower and was forced to reinstate the draft. In addition his prospects in the upcoming 1948 presidential election looked dim. Desperate to shore up his base in Northern urban areas, Truman began to develop a cautious civil rights agenda, including protection for black voting rights, antilynching legislation, and a permanent version of the Fair Employment Practice Committee that Roosevelt had put in place during World War II. Truman was also willing to entertain proposals for an integrated military, and met with Randolph and other black leaders for this purpose in March 1948. By then Randolph had formed the Committee to End Jim Crow in the Military, and Rustin had enlisted enthusiastically, ignoring for the moment the paradox presented by his pacifism. Rustin helped outline a plan to apply nonviolent direct action techniques to the armed forces. Enlisted men would refuse to obey orders relating to segregated practices, precipitating a mutiny. It was in this charged climate that Randolph met with Truman. Like Roosevelt, prior to the threatened March on Washington seven years earlier, Truman sought to jawbone Randolph into moderation. But as before, the civil rights leader stood firm. In testimony before Congress, Randolph advocated a black boycott of a segregated military.

On the surface, then, it seemed that Randolph and Rustin were of one mind. But as events transpired in the summer of 1948, it became clear they were not, leading to a lengthy personal estrangement and providing another example of the difficulties Rustin faced in reconciling his dreams. Although Randolph harbored pacifist sympathies, his primary goal was a racially integrated, economically egalitarian America. He criticized Truman harshly when the president signed a draft act in June that left segregation intact. He held rallies across the nation calling on African Americans to boycott the armed forces as long as they discriminated against them. He picketed against Truman in front of the White House. Randolph even supported Rustin when he formed a League for Nonviolent Civil Disobedience, which would actively recruit and organize draft resisters and protesters within the armed services, endangering his reputation as a patriot at a time when charges of "disloyalty" carried enormous weight.

But in 1948 Truman issued an executive order mandating equal treatment in the military. His acceptance of a civil rights platform at that year's Democratic National Convention had sparked a Southern delegate walkout led by South Carolina Governor Strom Thurmond. Reorganized as the States' Rights Democratic, or Dixiecrat Party, they nominated Thurmond for president. Truman now needed the support of Northern blacks and liberals more than ever, and his executive order represented an attempt to shore up his political base. Randolph had received what he wanted and called off his campaign. For him, this was a defining moment in the history of the struggle for civil rights in the United States, and enough to outweigh the president's pragmatic motives or any implications for peace and war.

It was not enough for Rustin, however. His agenda was much more ambitious. Rustin viewed Randolph's cause as only one part of a larger struggle against war and for a new society based on principles of peace, equality, and brotherhood. Although as a civil rights activist Rustin could demand a desegregated military, as a pacifist he rejected the military altogether. The evil of racial discrimination in the U.S. armed forces was secondary to the evil of the armed forces themselves. Rustin announced that his campaign of civil disobedience would continue. He even issued a press release in Randolph's name criticizing Truman's executive order, angering his mentor. It was two years before the men spoke again.

After Rustin's arrest in August 1948 for attempting to interfere with the draft process, his splinter movement petered out. Conscription was implemented, and by 1950, when the United States entered the Korean War, blacks and whites were fighting and dying together, small consolation to a man who dreamed of a world without armed conflict. Once again, Rustin had been forced to choose between his dreams. In 1941 he had chosen the cause of civil rights when it was threatened by the implications of his Communist affiliations. Now faced with the paradox of racial segregation in the military, an institution whose legitimacy he rejected, he reached the opposite conclusion. But this was akin to attempting to square a circle. Rustin's dreams were so inspired that they would not hold together; he was constantly being forced to leave pieces behind.

The campaign to integrate the military cost him personally, when he lost his father figure Randolph, and politically, because he burned bridges to civil rights activists who viewed him as a turncoat. The latter included Roy Wilkins (1901–1981), a rising leader within the NAACP and its future president, whose lifelong suspicion of Rustin dated from this controversy. The battle over a segregated military also revived the question of whether an American dream that sought to combine pacifism, socialism, and civil rights was viable in a nation in which the imperatives of race, class, and Cold War politics often led in different directions. The trials of the 1940s taught Rustin that what was good for African Americans was not necessarily good for pacifists, what was good for Marxists was not necessarily good for African Americans, and what was good for pacifists was not necessarily good for opponents of racism and bigotry. Over the next four decades, he would often sidestep these contradictions. He never fully resolved them.

Rustin spent the rest of the 1940s and the early 1950s immersed in the anticolonialist and world peace movements. He traveled to India in the wake of the death of Mahatma Gandhi, who had been assassinated in January 1948, to participate in a conference on pacifism and nonviolent direct action that the Indian leader had planned. The conference was canceled, but Rustin nonetheless made good use of his time there. In January and February 1949 he met with leaders of what had been the most successful nonviolent political movement in world history, including Gandhi's colleague and successor Jawaharlal Nehru. The visit served as a seminar on the philosophy and strategy of peaceful political change, one whose lessons would prove readily adaptable to racial conditions in the United States during the civil rights movement.

Rustin also sought to apply these lessons to the emerging anticolonialist movement in Africa. In 1952 he traveled to the British colonies of Nigeria and the Gold Coast (present-day Ghana) to meet with leaders of their independence movements. He left optimistic about the possibilities for replicating Gandhi's Indian success in Africa. The conditions on the ground appeared similar: an unpopular British regime, a restive population clamoring for self-determination, and charismatic local leaders, in this instance, Kwame Nkrumah of the Gold Coast and Nnamdi Azikiwe of Nigeria. Rustin counseled them to follow Gandhi's example of nonviolent political and social activism in an atmosphere of ethnic and religious inclusiveness.

Rustin visiting Indian leader Jawaharlal Nehru, 1949. Source: Estate of Bayard Rustin.

Both leaders seemed receptive at this relatively early stage of the West African anticolonialist struggle, but subsequent events would prove disappointing. Gandhi had always feared the corrosive effects of ethnic and religious divisions in India. With the forced partition of the country into Hindu and Muslim nations immediately after independence in 1947, his apprehensions were borne out. Rustin shared Gandhi's fear of chauvinism overpowering the shared humanity of those who employed nonviolence to effect social and political change. In time the independent nations of Nigeria and Ghana, fractured by sectarianism, offered more examples of its dangers. It was, however, the fissures between integrationists and separatists that developed in the U.S. civil rights movement during the late 1960s that affected him most deeply, by exposing the limitations of nonviolent direct action as a practical strategy.

These challenges lay in the future as Rustin's African tour came to an end in early 1953. Rustin was now well known within the pacifist community, but in view of its small size and limited influence, he was largely under the national radar. The Cold War, the arms race, and the Korean War ground on in the face of the pacifist movement he represented. Moreover, pacifists like Rustin were forced to defend themselves during this time against accusations of harboring communist sympathies, an ironic turn for someone with his political resume. As a socialist, Rustin supported democratic procedures, civil liberties, and the freedoms of speech, press, assembly, and religion. To his enemies in the Communist Party, these were all expendable in the interest of Marxist revolution. Rustin and his fellow socialists were also independent of the Soviet Union's dictates, which American communists obeyed unquestioningly. But as important as ideological distinctions were among American radicals—and few were more hostile toward communists than socialists—they were virtually meaningless to red baiters during the heyday of Joseph McCarthy in the early 1950s. Rustin, who believed deeply in democracy and who was second to none in his contempt for the Communist Party, nonetheless had generated a thick Federal Bureau of Investigation (FBI) file by 1953 merely by virtue of his position on disarmament, colonialism, civil rights, and economic justice.

This use of "guilt by association" to delegitimize dissenting voices such as Rustin's was typical of the Cold War political atmosphere. Arguments among Americans over communism channeled deeper anxieties over nuclear war, juvenile delinquency, race, gender relations, and family dynamics. The combination of homosexuality with political radicalism of any stripe was fraught with special danger, since gays were considered particularly vulnerable to blackmail by communist spies. Only weeks after his return from Africa, Rustin learned firsthand the perils of this aspect of Cold War paranoia.

In January 1953 the American Friends Service Committee sent Rustin to the West Coast for a series of speeches on world peace and anticolonialism. On the evening of January 21, he spoke in Pasadena, California. After the event, as was often his practice, he looked for male pickups on the side streets. Rustin was usually discreet enough to avoid the police, but on this night he was unlucky. He was found engaging in sex with two white males in a parked car and was arrested. On January 23 a Los Angeles judge sentenced him to sixty days in jail for performing a lewd act in a public venue. Rustin began serving his sentence immediately. Through a colleague, he offered Muste his profound apologies.

The FOR leader, however, was not in a forgiving mood. Prodigal sons can leave home once too often, and Muste felt he had been far too patient with his protégé. In addition to his sense of personal betrayal, Muste knew that FOR survived financially only through the generosity of donors who were deeply religious. To them, and to Muste as well, homosexuality was a biblical sin. Rustin had to leave. Muste requested and received his resignation from FOR, which the organization accepted formally on January 28. When Rustin completed his jail sentence in March 1953, he had nowhere to go.

The months after his release were among the lowest in Rustin's life. FOR had been his professional, emotional, and spiritual home for over eleven years. With this mooring gone he was adrift, struggling to come to terms with his sexuality, and more immediately, to earn a living. He consulted a psychiatrist at the behest of Muste, who viewed the sessions as "treatment" for Rustin's "illness." Given the prevailing national atmosphere of hostility and suspicion toward homosexuals, it is not surprising that Rustin told his therapist that his behavior was sinful. But he also maintained that it was part of who he was, and that he could not change. He promised only to be more careful and controlled in the future.

At the time, Rustin was struggling with the idea that his expression of love for a man was as legitimate as that of a man for a woman. A visionary in politics, Rustin was a man of his time in matters of sexual choice. In 1953 this meant accepting the prevailing view of his behavior. He did, however, continue to maintain relationships with men. He did not, like many homosexuals at the time, allow societal disapproval to push him into the surface trappings of "straight" life and the protections they offered. In this sense, while by no means a gay rights activist, Rustin refused to give in completely to prevailing assumptions and pressures. Linking the personal to the political would have to come later, but merely by holding to his sexual identity Rustin made as strong a statement as a gay man could at a time when even radical leftists like Muste could not fit homosexuality into their understandings of the world.

In the meantime Rustin searched for work in New York, where he had returned after his release from jail. AFSC had also cut him loose in the wake of his arrest, and he was forced to take a succession of menial jobs to make ends meet. Rustin spent the first half of 1953 in personal and professional hell. FOR had given him a work identity, a philosophy of life, and a close circle of friends. Now all were gone. Perhaps most heartbreaking was the loss of friendships. Men and women he had known and worked with for years at FOR now shunned him. Rustin collaborated with Muste in the succeeding years, but his paternal connection with the older man was gone. Clearly, there was no future for him in the religious wing of the pacifist movement. There was, however, another option, and it proved to be his deliverance.

The War Resisters League (WRL) had been founded after World War I as an international pacifist organization. It shared FOR's goals, but not its Christian orientation. The WRL was resolutely secular, appealing to political radicals of all persuasions who embraced nonviolence. Thus Rustin's "morals" conviction was less important to the WRL than to FOR. Rustin had worked with WRL-affiliated activists in the past, including some who had participated in the Journey of Reconciliation. Perhaps best of all for Rustin, the organization needed him. It was losing money and members, and its continued existence was in question. Clearly the WRL required someone with Rustin's abilities. In the fall of 1953, over the objections of Muste, who sat on the WRL's executive committee, the organization took him on as program director. In 1954 he was promoted to executive secretary. The WRL served as his base of operations until the mid-1960s. Although its atmosphere was not quite as close-knit as the familial FOR—there were no father figures here—the WRL gave Rustin a home once again. The organization made it possible for him to do some of the most significant work of his life, however, not in the area of peace but in civil rights. Only months after being reduced to working as a furniture mover, Rustin had his career back.

Rustin reinvigorated the WRL during the 1950s through his leadership, organizing skills, and flair for publicity. But his new organization was even smaller than FOR, and it struggled against a massive tide of Cold War–inspired popular opinion. The WRL made little headway in slowing the arms race during the Dwight D. Eisenhower administration, which was characterized by Secretary of State John Foster Dulles's use of the threat of nuclear destruction as a diplomatic tool against the Soviet Union. However, it did lay the groundwork for new leftist politics in the 1960s. Rustin and his WRL colleagues understood the connections between capitalism, imperialism, and militarism and sought to attack them with words and deeds. A notable example came on June 15, 1955, Operation Alert day across the United States, when all Americans were required to take shelter at a specified time during a simulated nuclear attack. Rustin led a WRL-sponsored protest in New York's City Hall Park, a location he selected deliberately for its dramatic effect. His refusal to go to a designated shelter area cost him more time in jail, but the WRL received national attention and, at least within the pacifist community, renewed respect.

A year later Rustin helped found the independent leftist journal *Liberation*, which articulated his critique of what would soon be known as America's "military-industrial complex." *Liberation* represented an attempt to create a non-Communist leftist voice in the United States that was not beholden to the Soviet "party line" on issues of civil rights, economic justice, civil liberties, and disarmament. This was no simple matter. The large degree of issue "overlap" between Communist and non-Communist leftists exposed the latter to guilt-by-association charges leveled by right-wing critics. But Rustin knew that what truly distinguished his brand of leftism from that of Communists was its consistent commitment to democratic practices, one that was independent of the twists and turns of the Soviet Union's foreign policy apparatus. *Liberation* was a means of making that distinction, as well as synthesizing a leftist politics that opposed war, racism, and the excesses of American capitalism without succumbing to the siren call of totalitarianism.

Rustin wrote extensively for the journal and served on its editorial board until the mid-1960s. By then it had become a leading organ of what was known as the New Left, a radicalism liberated from the connections with Soviet repression that had delegitimatized the older, Communist left. The New Left traced its origins to the birth in 1962 of Students for a Democratic Society (SDS), a group that brought the perspective of students and youth to American radicalism. In its founding document, the Port Huron Statement, SDS challenged the United States to live up to its stated ideals of equality, freedom, and democracy and to resolve the contradictions that lay beneath them. The

New Left's analysis of these contradictions was a powerful indictment of racism, poverty, militarism, and imperialism in contemporary American life. It owed much to Rustin, the WRL, and *Liberation*. The road to the New Left of the 1960s began in the 1950s, when Rustin and a small group of colleagues on the fringes of the American political landscape assembled out of disparate parts of the "old" left ideas and arguments that would alter that landscape profoundly. Although this new radicalism became popular in the 1960s, in the mid-1950s there seemed little chance of any such transformation occurring. Rustin trudged on at the helm of a shoestring organization of the American left, measuring his successes in small increments. Facing indifference from its potential audience at best and outright hostility at worst, the peace movement as a whole seemed locked in place.

But at the same time, the nation's racial atmosphere was changing profoundly. World War II had made it impossible to ignore the gross inequities of race in America. The glaring hypocrisy of a nation victorious in a battle against racism overseas, permitting it to exist within its own borders, was lost on few outside the white South. During and immediately after the war, thousands of African Americans streamed into Northern cities seeking industrial jobs, in what was known as the Second Great Migration; a smaller one had occurred during World War I. This population shift placed the issue of civil rights immediately before Democratic Party politicians, who coveted black votes. The combination of self-interest and high principle that typifies American electoral politics led these politicians to incorporate black voters into their constituencies. This in turn produced a group of African American elected officials, such as Congressmen Adam Clayton Powell of New York and William Dawson of Chicago, who not only wielded power locally but ensured that the issue of Southern racism would reach a Northern as well as international audience.

They were aided in this effort by the Cold War, which offered the Soviet Union a rich propaganda opportunity in its competition with the United States for the allegiance of developing, largely nonwhite nations. The Soviet Union sought to exploit the existence of Jim Crow in the South to discredit its Cold War rival and claim moral superiority. Even the most racially callous U.S. government officials were deeply concerned with the outcome of the Cold War and with the effect that racial injustice might have on it. Thus, the Cold War contributed to the changing American civil rights culture in the decade immediately following World War II.

But the impact of World War II, the Cold War, and the Second Great Migration might not have been enough to begin the modern civil rights era if not for the ongoing legal efforts of the NAACP. W. E. B. Du Bois and others had founded the NAACP in 1910, at a low point in African American history. The infamous *Plessy v. Ferguson* Supreme Court decision of 1896, which declared "separate but equal" public accommodations constitutional, had given legal sanction to an array of Jim Crow laws that segregated schools, theaters, parks, hotels, and street cars, and effectively disenfranchised black voters. Beginning in the 1930s, the NAACP brought a series of federal lawsuits through its Legal Defense Fund that were designed to bring down *Plessy's* edifice of "separate but equal." This effort accelerated after World War II, as the Legal Defense Fund, led by future Supreme Court Justice Thurgood Marshall, sought a high Court ruling that all separate facilities were inherently unequal. In the early 1950s Marshall began to press the claim of Linda Brown, a black Topeka, Kansas, girl who had been denied admission to a "white" school in her neighborhood.

By the time *Brown v. Board of Education* reached the Supreme Court in 1953, the body had a new chief justice, Earl Warren, who was ready to steer it in a new direction. President Eisenhower had appointed Warren in the hope of effecting a conservative shift in the high tribunal, but in an example of historical irony, he instead led it into a liberal activist phase. Under Warren, the Court sought to regulate everyday relationships between individuals in local communities, relationships that the *Plessy* majority had insisted were private and beyond the reach of federal judges. On May 17, 1954, a unanimous Court ruled in *Brown v. Board of Education* that no amount of spending could make Linda Brown's all-black Topeka, Kansas, elementary school "equal" to the all-white school from which she was barred. Separation was inherently unequal. By implication this meant that all racially segregated public venues, including buses, trains, hotels, restaurants, and parks, were also unconstitutional.

Although the Court was vague regarding the timetable for enforcing its decision—"all deliberate speed" was its cryptic 1955 prescription—it was clear that the ground had shifted in American race relations. The national mood and the Supreme Court had come together in a way that made the overthrow of a Jim Crow system that had frozen the South in time for three quarters of a century a distinct hope. The high Court's reluctance to implement its own decision presented the South's African American population with both a burden and an opportunity. If the walls of racial segregation were to come down, they would have to provide the muscle themselves. Yet the Southern social system, itself sustained by violence, was not susceptible to force. Strong government enforcement initiatives were not in the immediate offing. It was thus that nonviolent direct action, a philosophy and strategy that had occupied a small corner of the American Left, was poised to become the instrument of racial liberation in the United States. Its engineers would be a young Baptist minister in Montgomery, Alabama, named Martin Luther King, Jr., and his mentor, Bayard Rustin.

On December 1, 1955, Rosa Parks, a seamstress and active member of the Alabama chapter of the NAACP, refused to give up her seat to a white man on a Montgomery bus as part of a prearranged plan. After the driver called the police, she was arrested. Four days later, a group of black ministers, labor leaders, educators, and everyday folk began a yearlong boycott of the city bus system that would enter historical legend as the opening blow of the modern U.S. civil rights movement. It also marked the emergence of Martin Luther King, Jr., as the movement's leader, public face, and symbol.

As spokesman for the newly formed Montgomery Improvement Association, organized to coordinate the boycott, King confronted a white power structure desperate to preserve its prerogatives and willing to employ desperate measures to do so. Over the course of the previous one hundred years, the institutional framework of white supremacy in the South had developed into a monolith. Police, elected officials, judges, voting registrars, the penal system, business associations, "citizens' councils," even extralegal terror groups such as the Ku Klux Klan all worked together to ensure that the racial status quo remained in place. King was all too familiar with this framework of intimidation and knew what the fledgling boycott was up against. He also understood the personal risks he was taking and had initially been reluctant to assume a leadership role for this reason. King, however, was indispensable to the moment, even if he did not fully comprehend this himself.

King was the son of one of the most powerful black preachers in the South. He had grown up in Atlanta absorbing the cadences, homilies, and rhetoric of the African American church that shaped his own speaking style as an adult. From the beginning, King was groomed to succeed his father and assume his mantle in Atlanta's black community. But graduate school and seminary in the North in the early 1950s would alter his trajectory. His teachers and mentors, who had in turn been influenced by Mahatma Gandhi, exposed King to the principles of nonviolent social change. By the time he assumed his first ministerial post in Montgomery in 1954, intending it as merely a way station on his road back to Atlanta and his father's pulpit, the idea of nonviolence and the momentum of the civil rights movement were about to meet. And Rustin made this possible. King had read about the principles of nonviolent direct action. But Rustin had lived them. There was much that Rustin could teach King, and thanks to Randolph he would get his chance.

King understood that while the success of the Montgomery boycott would hinge primarily on the unity and determination of the city's black population, he would also need strategic and financial help from the North. With Rustin's assistance, he received both. In February 1956, with the boycott already endangered by white violence and harassment, Randolph convened a meeting of civil rights leaders and pacifists in New York who decided that Rustin should go south to assist King. Rustin and Randolph had also recently formed another group called In Friendship to raise money for the civil rights movement in the South. It procured funds primarily from liberal labor unions, including Randolph's

Sleeping Car Porters, the International Ladies' Garment Workers Union, the United Packinghouse Workers, and various government employee organizations. The timing thus could not have been better for the Montgomery boycott. In Friendship began to funnel cash to King and the Montgomery Improvement Association, rectifying at least to some degree what had traditionally been a racially skewed distribution of financial resources in the South. In Friendship also established a strong nexus of mutual support between organized labor and the civil rights movement, forming the elements of an interracial, class-based alliance that was at the heart of Rustin's American dream. In his lifelong effort to bring the two together, In Friendship was one of his great successes.

The Martin Luther King, Jr., that Rustin met when he arrived in Montgomery in February 1956 was not yet the figure of myth and memory. Unsure of himself, concerned for his family's physical safety after his house was fire bombed in January, he was a powerful spokesman for the boycott but lacked a clear understanding of its deeper meaning and final destination. Despite his exposure to Gandhian principles, he had not yet made an explicit connection between nonviolence, civil rights, and transformative social change. There were, in fact, guns in King's house when Rustin first visited; Rustin saw one on a chair as a colleague began to sit down and half-humorously warned him away.

Notwithstanding, Rustin and King bonded almost immediately and remained close until the latter's death. As with Randolph, Rustin supplied an element missing in King's life. Despite his Northern education, King in 1956 was very much a product of the insular black South. There was much in the "outside" world he had not seen or experienced. Rustin was his link to that world. With his erect bearing, clipped accent, and air of calm confidence, he gave the appearance of one who had traveled in sophisticated and influential circles and could navigate them for the younger man. Unlike King, Rustin always seemed to know what to do. He possessed what King lacked at the time: a program, based on nonviolence, that allowed him to respond to events in a measured, coherent way. King quickly came to look up to Rustin, if not as a father figure, then as a respected, worldly uncle.

For his part, Rustin, having been a son to Randolph and Muste, welcomed a chance to be a mentor himself, especially to a protégé with the intelligence and character of King. But beyond this, Rustin viewed King as the medium of his own dreams, a man who could accomplish what he—an ex-Communist, a draft resister, and a convicted "sex offender"—could not. Rustin knew that after years of political marginality, nonviolence could become relevant to the entire nation through King. The bus boycott offered the opportunity for African Americans to use nonviolent direct action to straighten the crooked path of American race relations, first in Montgomery, then in the South, and finally, in the nation as a whole. Simultaneously, King could be at the heart of a combined civil rights and labor movement that sought both racial and economic justice in the United States. King, then, was the man on whom Rustin could project his own American dream of a nation without poverty, racism, or war.

Rustin spent hours with King, often late at night after busy days of organizing and marching. He made him see that arrests provided an opportunity to expose the injustices of the local "justice" system, and that harassment of boycotters as they walked or drove to work revealed the violence that underlay the Jim Crow system to the rest of the nation. The African American drivers and walkers who responded nonviolently to the provocations of the white authorities were the pioneers of a mass antiracist movement. Theirs could be a new community, bound together by a creed that was empowering and liberating. All the protesters needed, Rustin told King, was the discipline not to strike back physically at the manifestations of injustice and the inner strength to empathize with their oppressors. If they held to that discipline and that inner strength, they would win.

The tenor of the boycott began to change almost from the moment Rustin arrived in Montgomery. He wrote a powerful address for King on the ways of nonviolence and its capacity to overcome hatred, which gave the protest a clear moral center. On Rustin's advice, when boycott leaders were indicted and arrested, they gave themselves up voluntarily as living witnesses to injustice. Rustin employed his musical skills to write and sing protest songs, infusing familiar spirituals with new, topical lyrics. He also helped organize a day in which all boycotters walked to their destinations, creating a dramatic effect that attracted national media attention.

Rustin's influence on the boycott continued through its successful conclusion in December 1956, long after his departure from Montgomery. His time in the city, in fact, had been relatively short. He immediately drew the attention of local authorities—a tall, elegant black man with an obvious air of authority could not fail to do so—and they began investigating the background of this "outsider." Randolph, under pressure from pacifist and socialist leaders fearful that Rustin would damage the boycott's credibility, reluctantly called him back to New York after a little more than a week in Montgomery. But the impact of his time in Alabama would be felt for decades afterward in the life and work of King. Thanks to Rustin, Montgomery was not an end in itself, but a beginning, for both a man and a movement.

Back home in New York, Rustin continued to work on behalf of the boycott. He was probably the individual most responsible for bringing it to the attention of Northern whites, publishing an account of his experiences titled "Montgomery Diary" in *Liberation*, ghost-writing an article by King, and attracting coverage in the mainstream white media. His most important contribution was organizing a huge Madison Square Garden rally in support of the boycott in May 1956. The rally drew almost twenty thousand New Yorkers and ended in the early morning hours. It was a classic Rustin production, uniting labor (the Sleeping Car Porters and the International Ladies' Garment Workers were major sponsors), civil rights (the NAACP was another sponsor, and Congressman Adam Clayton Powell gave the keynote address), and white liberals (Eleanor Roosevelt made a well-publicized appearance).

Looking out over the crowd, Rustin could not help but feel the contrast between it and the small group of pacifists to which he had devoted the past fifteen years of his life. FOR, WRL, and AFSC combined could not have drawn a tenth of this audience. The seeds of Rustin's advocacy of compromise and coalition politics may have begun to gestate here. Ten years earlier, he was serving time in a federal prison for resisting a war effort led by Franklin D. Roosevelt. Now he was joining with the late president's widow as a colleague, an ally in a common cause. And the cause—the Montgomery boycott—was on its way to victory. World War II, of course, had ground on in spite of his sacrifices, almost in mockery of them. Was it preferable to accomplish what he could from within the political mainstream, building bridges to those with different views in hopes of making incremental progress, or continue as the proud, pure dissenter? As he sat in the wings at Madison Square Garden watching Eleanor Roosevelt that night in May 1956, the answer to this question was beginning to take shape in his mind.

The Montgomery bus boycott ended successfully in December 1956 when the Supreme Court affirmed a lower federal court ruling declaring segregated seating on city buses unconstitutional. The city's black community had stayed the course for over a year, to the amazement of white Southerners, as well as quite a few Northerners. King was now a national figure, thanks to his eloquence and courage, not to mention Rustin's guidance. But King had received another piece of assistance from his mentor that would create complications for him down the road. During the boycott, Rustin introduced King to Stanley Levison, a wealthy white New York businessman with a strong interest in civil rights. Levison soon became one of King's closest advisers, as well as a major financial contributor. However, like Rustin, Levison carried unwelcome baggage. A longtime member of the Communist Party, Levison was a potential source of embarrassment to King and other civil rights leaders who felt they had enough difficulties without the added burdens of guilt by association. By necessity King kept his relationship with Levison away from prying eyes. Nonetheless, if King's longtime colleague Ralph Abernathy was his public alter ego, Levison and Rustin filled this role in private. It is doubtful that King would have developed as he did without them. King's combination of moral leadership, philosophical rigor, and political acumen bore the clear stamp of these two outcasts.

An illustration of Rustin's ambivalent position in King's life came immediately after the triumph of the Montgomery boycott, when the two began planning a permanent organization that would apply the techniques of nonviolent direct action to other venues. The new group would be called the Southern Christian Leadership Conference (SCLC), and although King became its president and public face, Rustin shaped its purpose and vision. In a set of organizational blueprints prepared with Levison, he urged that the SCLC reach beyond nonviolent mass protest and build alliances with sympathetic white liberals and union officials, so that it could attack the intertwined issues of racism, poverty, and workers' rights. It would thus be an organization capable of operating both outside the established order, in its use of direct action, and inside it, through contacts with political and labor leaders and the pursuit of electoral rights. The blueprints represented another of Rustin's steps toward mainstream politics and the types of compromises that would have been unthinkable during his years in federal prison.

Rustin's work laid the foundation for the SCLC, which was formally launched by King, Abernathy, and other Southern black clergymen early in 1957. By 1960 Rustin was head of the SCLC's New York office, as well as a special assistant to King. But Rustin angered turf-conscious NAACP President Roy Wilkins in June of that year with a plan to stage civil rights demonstrations at the 1960 Democratic and Republican National Conventions. Wilkins, moderate in his politics but militant in his disapproval of Rustin's sexuality, conspired with the equally prejudiced black Congressman Adam Clayton Powell of New York to discredit him. A power broker in the African American political community who was jealous of threats to his primacy, Powell spread rumors that Rustin and King were engaged in a homosexual affair—a red flag to the culturally conservative ministers of the SCLC. A mortified King backed away from Rustin, who was forced to resign both as King's assistant and from the SCLC. Over the next few years, King would sometimes write to Rustin or use him for back channel consultation, but remained fearful about the possibility of his "history" rubbing off on him. The two did not resume their public association until 1963 and the March on Washington.

Other civil rights leaders also engaged in this self-serving treatment. Wilkins, for example, was happy to have Rustin help organize a 1957 Prayer Pilgrimage to Washington, D.C., demanding that the federal government enforce the *Brown* decision, but on other occasions when he deemed such assistance unnecessary, Wilkins argued that Rustin was too "hot" to touch. Although Rustin never complained publicly, he was grievously wounded by this ostracism, especially when it involved King. Rustin was acutely aware of his special abilities. He would probably have concurred with the government official who said he was one of the five most intelligent men in the United States.[1] A sense of wasted opportunity gnawed at him during his periods of exile. It seemed that leftists who did not hesitate to criticize the close-mindedness of their political enemies were not immune to it themselves. The hypocrisies of Powell and King, both active womanizers, in criticizing Rustin's own sex life could not have been lost on him. There was also the altogether human temptation to reject those who had rejected him when they returned in their time of need. But Rustin always responded—to King, to Wilkins, even to Powell, a corrupt self-aggrandizer—because the causes that animated his life outweighed all else. That those causes were political, economic, and social, but not until the last years of his life cultural in nature meant that personal melodrama had no place in his relationships with those he considered partners in struggle. Forgiveness thus came more easily to him than most.

Regardless of his disappointments at the hands of civil rights leaders, Rustin had a secure home within the U.S. peace movement during the late 1950s and early 1960s. His colleagues at the WRL seemed ever willing to lend him out to other movements and bring him back into the fold after his work there had run its course. Although there was significant overlap between the peace and civil rights movements, there was also tension between the two regarding Rustin, who was valuable to both. Randolph and Muste, his two mentors, symbolized this struggle for allegiance.

Randolph viewed the years following the Montgomery boycott as critical for African Americans. The *Brown* case was law but required enforcement all over the South, and the 1956 "Southern Manifesto," a denunciation of the Supreme Court decision signed by virtually every Southern member of Congress, promised that this would be a long and difficult process. The Little Rock crisis of 1957, in which state and local officials in Arkansas fought a federal school desegregation court order so strenuously that President Eisenhower, while no friend of *Brown*, felt compelled to send in the 101st Airborne Division to reaffirm its authority, exemplified this regionwide defiance. That year also saw the passage of the first federal civil rights act in almost a century. It created a Civil Rights Division in the Department of Justice devoted to enforcing voting rights, but it relied on individual complaints from blacks. Thus, like *Brown*, the act was not self-executing.

The SCLC sought to be proactive, sponsoring a 1958 Crusade for Citizenship to enfranchise Southern blacks, which Rustin helped organize. The crusade targeted black neighborhoods in which voter participation rates were near zero for workshops and registration drives led by local SCLC-affiliated clergymen. Rustin believed that hundreds of thousands of new black voters in the South could destroy the region's Jim Crow past and remake it in the image of equality and brotherhood. Inspired by this environment so ripe with possibility, Randolph believed that history was turning, and that the battle for racial equality thus took precedence over all others. Organized pacifism—small numbers of well-meaning but naive idealists staging arrests at military installations and nuclear facilities without significantly altering the course of the arms race— seemed to him weak and ineffectual by comparison.

But Muste, with whom Rustin had reconciled professionally by the late 1950s, thought otherwise. A lifelong civil rights activist—it was he, after all, who had sponsored CORE—Muste still believed in the primacy of the peace issue. And with Cold War hysteria at its peak and nuclear weapons proliferating globally, the clock of armageddon seemed to be approaching midnight. Peace, of course, meant more than the mere absence of war. A peaceful world would also be one in which racism and economic inequality did not exist. But to the veteran radical, now past seventy, peace was the epicenter of the moral universe, and if only a few true believers shared this view, then so be it. A life spent in defiance of a misguided majority, even if filled with symbolic gestures, was nevertheless a life well spent. Muste wanted Rustin to continue the work of peace, even in the face of indifference and abuse. It was the most important work of all.

Thus Rustin once again faced a choice between two essential elements of his dream for America, which in this instance were not so much diametrically opposed as competitors for his attention and time. But they also represented a deeper dilemma between the stance of the principled outsider and the practical insider in American political life. Principled pacifism offered purity of spirit and the satisfactions of the symbolic deed, but civil rights activism, fraught with pragmatic compromise and the disappointments of the partially achieved objective, still promised to change the nation in a tangible, palpable way. A younger Rustin had unhesitatingly chosen principle over compromise. But now in middle age, he began to edge away from the politics of gesture and toward a realism that perhaps could only have come from one who had paid so high a price for his unwillingness to bend to the prevailing winds. It may well be that pacifism ceased to be the preeminent cause of his life because of the emergence of King and the opportunities presented by the new landscape of race in the America of the late 1950s. But he also may have come to a rueful acceptance of the limitations of his pacifism: so much time and sacrifice, and so little to show for it. An older and less headstrong Rustin began to engage more closely with civil rights, as well as the art of the possible.

The disappointments of pacifist activism in the late 1950s heightened Rustin's sense of frustration. In April 1958 he traveled to Europe for a disarmament campaign sponsored by a newly formed umbrella group of peace organizations, the Committee for Nonviolent Action. The trip was unique in that it included a planned stop in Moscow. Rustin understood that the protest would lack credibility if it was perceived as directed solely against Western European democracies, and he also wished to emphasize his own anticommunist sensibilities. The campaign got off to a promising start in London, from which Rustin marched with a crowd of ten thousand to Aldermatson, the headquarters of the British nuclear program. From there his group passed through other continental cities, with mixed results. They failed to generate interest in Paris, awash in a hypernationalistic reaction to the Algerian independence movement. The Soviets stonewalled the protesters when they tried to enter the country, stranding them in Helsinki without entry visas, and the campaign ended inconclusively.

A year later Rustin embarked on an even more dramatic crusade, this time an attempt to prevent France from engaging in atomic testing in its Algerian colony. The action involved flying to Ghana and traveling over two thousand miles north to the French testing site in the desert. The trip allowed him to renew acquaintances with Kwame Nkrumah, by that time prime minister of an independent Ghana, but the protest itself, hamstrung by logistical impediments, did not achieve its goal. In December 1959 and again in January 1960 Rustin's group was intercepted by French authorities at border crossings and turned away. France's nuclear tests proceeded as scheduled.

As the 1960s began Rustin remained the WRL's executive secretary, but pacifism no longer played the role in his life that it had during the preceding two decades. Nonviolence now had more meaning in the context of civil rights, where it was proving its power and effectiveness. In February 1960 four black students at North Carolina A&T College in Greensboro, North Carolina, staged a pro-integration sit-in at a segregated Woolworth's lunch counter. They sparked a wave of similar actions across the upper South that made significant inroads against Jim Crow in public facilities and in some instances integrated entire downtown business districts. The success of nonviolent direct action techniques during the sit-ins inspired the formation of the Student Nonviolent Coordinating Committee (SNCC) later that year. Rustin was one of the few "adults" permitted to advise this group, composed of students wishing to employ grassroots activity, including civil disobedience, to destroy white supremacy in the South.

SNCC's founders had deliberately distanced themselves from King, who had originally planned to use the group as SCLC's youth arm. But the students distrusted the kind of charismatic, "top-down" leadership that King offered. They intended instead to create a community of equals that took the fight for freedom into the towns and villages of the rural South. SNCC organized on the grassroots level, doing the long-term, dangerous work for which King, with his demanding schedule, had neither the time nor the inclination. Over the next five years, SNCC voting rights projects in Alabama and Mississippi were decisive in enfranchising the African American population of those states.

Rustin's hopes for a permanent position with SNCC were dashed by concerns about his background and the lingering effects of the Powell-generated rumor of a Rustin-King affair. SNCC's leaders may have been younger than those in the SCLC, but they were just as uncomfortable with homosexuality. Rustin still had the satisfaction of playing a major role in the creation of an organization whose members used nonviolence in socially transformative ways, as he himself had done in the past. Now, however, in the place of a few dozen pacifists, there were thousands of young idealists, the hinge on which history might turn.

Rustin was also encouraged by the Freedom Rides, which took place in the spring of 1961, and paid homage to the Journey of Reconciliation fourteen years earlier, in which Rustin had played a central role. Interstate transportation facilities were still segregated in the South, Supreme Court pronouncements notwithstanding, and an interracial group of CORE activists, led by James Farmer, embarked once again to challenge the status quo. This time, however, they set their sights not on the upper South, but on the hard-core states of Alabama and Mississippi, where racial mores were much more likely to be leavened with violence. Almost predictably, the Freedom Riders were only a few miles past the state line in Anniston, Alabama, when their bus was fire bombed by a white mob. CORE was forced to discontinue the rides after its members were brutally beaten at the Birmingham bus terminal, but SNCC activists took up the campaign and rode as far as Jackson, Mississippi. In the fall of 1961 the Interstate Commerce Commission issued regulations that finally desegregated public transportation in the South, completing the work Rustin had begun a decade and a half earlier. Unlike the Journey of Reconciliation, the Freedom Rides received national attention; CORE was now a household name. Even with no official connection to the organization, Rustin felt vindicated by its success. Nonviolent direct action was now the engine of a civil rights movement, which itself was moving to the center of American political and social life.

Rustin also had the opportunity to defend nonviolent direct action as a philosophy during a debate tour with the Black Muslim leader Malcolm X later in 1961 and in 1962. Malcolm, a passionate critic of both the integrationist ethos and nonviolence, was a feared debater, known for his ability to portray mainstream civil rights leaders as "Uncle Toms." But Rustin was a skilled debater himself and could remind his younger opponent that he had begun fighting for black equality when Malcolm was a child. He was also able to present, in ways that Malcolm could not, a coherent vision for black America. It was built around redistribution of economic resources and a democratic socialism that was much more radical in its implications than anything the Nation of Islam leader, whose disciples practiced a form of black capitalism, could offer. Most media accounts of the debates stressed the divisions between the two men over integration. Less remarked upon was the irony of the ostensibly more "moderate" Rustin mounting sharp criticisms of the inequities of capitalist economic development.

The debates with Malcolm X allowed Rustin more than the opportunity to disabuse his mostly black audiences of the notion that he was an "Uncle Tom." He was also able to show that an apostle of nonviolence could nonetheless be a revolutionary, and that a program built around interracialism and economic redistribution could be as radically transformative as one based on separatism and threats of violence. This theme would characterize King's final years as well, as he planned what became the Poor People's Campaign of 1968.

Yet, as 1962 ended, Rustin was still on the fringes. The civil rights movement had adopted his ideas, but not him. The pacifist movement had accepted him, but was itself marginalized. King, Wilkins, Muste, and others in both movements respected him but kept their distance, wary of the controversy that surrounded him. "Communist." "Draft dodger." "Deviant." It seemed that Rustin would never escape those labels. His years in the shadows, however, were about to end, thanks to an older man's dream and the events of the most important single day in civil rights history.

Note

1. Daniel Levine, *Bayard Rustin and the Civil Rights Movement* (New Brunswick, NJ: Rutgers University Press, 2000), pp. 3–4.

CHAPTER THREE

~

The March on Washington, 1963

Throughout his trials, Bayard Rustin could always count on A. Philip Randolph. Others might come and go, but the aging labor chief never wavered in his support. It was thus fitting that Randolph initiated Rustin's emergence as a national civil rights figure. It began with an informal meeting between the two in December 1962. Randolph recalled the March on Washington he had organized and then canceled two decades earlier. He had always harbored some regrets about his actions in 1941. Now he and Rustin observed that many of the same conditions that had inspired the calling of the initial demonstration persisted. The African American unemployment rate continued to outstrip that of whites. Job discrimination was still rampant. But the existence of substantial numbers of unemployed Americans, regardless of race, was what troubled the two men most. As democratic socialists, they had long dreamed of a federal jobs program that guaranteed employment to every American.

At times it had seemed as if this were close at hand. In 1944 President Roosevelt had delivered what became known as the "Second Bill of Rights" speech, in which he argued for an expanded definition of what government owed its citizens. The first ten amendments to the Constitution protected "procedural" rights, such as freedom of speech, assembly, and the press, but offered no "substantive" guarantees—of a job, an income, or medical care. Roosevelt proposed to obligate the federal government to provide these and other services, constructing a social safety net that would entitle every American to a basic standard of living and a rough equality of economic condition. FDR died before submitting a legislative program to Congress, but in 1946 liberal Democrats introduced a Full Employment Bill as a first step toward his goal. Denounced by

Republicans and conservative Democrats as a form of socialism, it passed only in a watered-down version that encouraged job creation but did not provide full employment.

Despite this disappointment, Randolph and Rustin continued to work toward a universal jobs program that, more than any other measure, embodied their democratic socialist agenda. They decided at their December 1962 meeting to try again, in the form of a new March on Washington, a civil rights demonstration for economic rights. In the twilight of his career, Randolph was getting another chance. So, for that matter, was Rustin. After decades on the margins, he would be at the center of what promised to be the largest demonstration in civil rights history, that is, if other civil rights leaders would support it. After years spent searching for ways to promote class-based interracialism on the American left, here was a momentous opportunity. The two men began to plan and organize.

Things started slowly. Rustin wanted the major civil rights organizations to pledge their support before making a public announcement of the march. He also needed financial contributions. By April 1963 CORE and SNCC had agreed to participate, but their coffers were largely empty. King and the Southern Christian Leadership Conference, also perennially cash-strapped, signed on in May. But the NAACP, headed by the imperious Roy Wilkins, no friend of Rustin, had the civil rights movement's largest membership base and its deepest pockets. Wilkins was hesitant. The NAACP had built its reputation challenging Jim Crow in the court system. Its leadership viewed mass demonstrations and civil disobedience—Rustin's strategies of choice—as misguided, even vaguely unsavory. And Rustin had originally planned the march as a two-day event that would include demonstrations on Capitol Hill and the possibility of congressional office sit-ins. This, along with Wilkins's opinion of Rustin as a dangerous "undesirable," led the NAACP leader to stall when asked for a commitment. Whitney Young, director of the National Urban League, who enjoyed close ties to the white business community and Washington officialdom, was similarly disinclined to join the march. Rustin and Randolph were faced with the prospect of proceeding without the support of the country's two most powerful civil rights organizations.

But events quickly took on a momentum of their own, sweeping the hesitant along with them. In April 1963 King and the SCLC launched a campaign to desegregate the downtown business district of Birmingham, Alabama, the most violently racist city in America. Over the next two months the entire nation saw, via the medium of television, the utter viciousness of the Southern Jim Crow system. King encouraged schoolchildren to join the marches that jammed the streets, and Birmingham's head of police, Eugene "Bull" Connor, responded by unleashing police dogs and fire hoses on protesters as young as six.

Amid the brutality and mass arrests, national public opinion shifted in the direction of the civil rights movement. One of the aims of nonviolent direct action was to expose gross injustice to onlookers of goodwill, and Connor obliged generously. His arrest of King himself became the occasion for the composition of the civil rights movement's defining text, the "Letter from Birmingham Jail." In the letter, King connected nonviolent direct action to an American tradition of legitimate protest, and, even more important, linked the black struggle for equality to the nation's founding principles. Composed on scraps of newspaper in one of the South's most notorious prisons, it made its author an American Gandhi, a powerful symbol of morality and justice and redeemer of 350 years of racial agony for his people and the nation. King's Nobel Peace Prize of the next year, marking his emergence as the world's leading spokesman for nonviolence and racial equality, was a direct result of the Birmingham campaign and of that letter.

Birmingham convinced Rustin that King must be the centerpiece of the March on Washington. As one who had spent his life outside the mainstream, Rustin understood that only King had the charisma and name recognition to force the march into the national consciousness. With every Bull Connor–inspired act of brutality in Birmingham, King's star rose. The events at Birmingham also affected President John F. Kennedy. He had been hesitant to throw the full weight of his office behind the civil rights movement for fear of losing Southern Democratic support and diverting attention from the Cold War. But by early June, Kennedy could no longer ignore the events in Birmingham, as well as attempts by white rioters to prevent the federal court-ordered registration of black students at the University of Alabama. On June 11 he addressed the nation. Declaring that racial equality presented "a moral issue" that was "as old as the Scriptures and . . . as clear as the American Constitution," he announced that he would submit a sweeping civil rights bill to Congress that would ban segregated public accommodations, employment discrimination, and interference with voting rights.[1]

The bill Kennedy proposed promised to be the most important piece of civil rights legislation in nearly a century. The Civil Rights Act of 1875, passed as Reconstruction was drawing to a close, had similarly prohibited separate public facilities but was held unconstitutional by the Supreme Court eight years later. Now Kennedy was determined to use federal power to reach into the daily lives of black and white Southerners. Jim Crow had always been sustained by the ability of state and local government entities to block federal intrusions. The Kennedy bill would obliterate those barriers and transform the social and political structures of the region. Aware of what was at stake, white Southerners readied for a desperate effort to stop the bill in Congress. Thanks to the seniority system and one-party rule, most committee chairmen were Southern Democrats. Moreover, while outnumbered in both Houses, Southern legislators were still numerous enough to filibuster the bill and prevent it from coming to a vote on the floor.

The Birmingham campaign and the civil rights bill, then, offered both risk and reward. If King could strike a hard blow at Jim Crow in Birmingham, the city that more than any other symbolized Southern racism, it would mark a turning point in the civil rights movement. If he failed, the entire movement could fail along with him. If legislation of this magnitude succeeded, a historic moment might be seized. If it did not, years and even decades might pass before such a moment would come again. It had, after all, been eighty-eight years since the Civil Rights Act of 1875. The March on Washington now took on added importance. It could serve as the locus of a massive lobbying effort to pass the Kennedy bill. With the stakes raised, Wilkins and Young scampered on board, putting aside their reservations about the value and appropriateness of mass civil rights demonstrations. By late June, Rustin had the unity, organizational muscle, and financial resources he needed.

But he also knew that the tone of the march had to change with the addition of the NAACP and Urban League. Rustin and Randolph were socialists, but Wilkins and Young were not. A march for economic equality—for a national jobs program and a guaranteed minimum income—was essentially one for a socialist agenda. But the civil rights bill did not concern itself directly with economic justice. It would give African Americans the right to eat at a restaurant, but not the money to pay for the meal. But perhaps, Rustin thought, after centuries on the outside looking in, this was enough for the moment. Legal rights by themselves would not guarantee racial justice in America, but they were essential steps along the way. Political equality would hasten economic justice. Sit-ins at congressional offices, moreover, were clearly not part of the NAACP's and Urban League's modus operandi, and this aspect of the march would have to be scaled back as well. Rustin could see that the addition of the two most powerful civil rights organizations would require him to limit the scope of his dreams.

Twenty years earlier, Rustin would have rejected compromise and insisted on occupying the moral high ground regardless of the consequences. But now he was more willing to give in. He was fifty-one years old and had been an activist—for peace, for socialism, for civil rights—almost half his life. Where had his efforts led? He was not well known except along the fringes of American radicalism and in the precincts of the FBI. The United States had prosecuted World War II without him. The Cold War continued unabated. There was no federal employment program, no national guaranteed income, and no universal health care system. The South remained segregated. Most of its African American population was still disenfranchised. The March on Washington would not remedy these injustices by itself, but it was a major undertaking that, with the addition of the NAACP and Urban League, promised to have a national impact. Virtually all segments of the black community were united behind it. White liberals, church groups, and labor unions were beginning to express interest. And with King, Wilkins, and other African American leaders reluctant even to mention his name in public, Rustin sensed that this might be his last chance to make a difference in America. Life on the "inside" might yield what the "outside" had not.

Rustin agreed to deprioritize the economic component of the march and build it primarily around the Kennedy civil rights bill. The bill proposed merely to secure rights already guaranteed by the Constitution. Most white Americans outside the South agreed that blacks were entitled to equal protection under the law. The Fourteenth Amendment itself was clear on this matter, as was the Fifteenth Amendment with regard to voting rights. But economic justice in the United States, as Rustin knew, was another matter. Relatively few whites in any part of the country endorsed the measures necessary to achieve a substantive equality of economic condition. Most American politicians, even liberals, were reluctant to employ the word "redistribution." Yet this is exactly what would be necessary to realize Rustin's agenda. The road to economic equality in the United States would thus be more treacherous than any other.

Rustin had not surrendered his hopes, but older and perhaps more world weary, he would hold to long-term dreams while accepting short-term gains. If the March on Washington succeeded in passing the civil rights bill, black and white Americans, for the first time in the nation's history, would have the right to eat at the same restaurants, stay at the same hotels, use the same restrooms, sit in adjoining seats on buses, trains, and theaters, swim at the same beaches, and cast the same ballots in primaries and elections. Thus blacks would, insofar as the public functions of American society were concerned, receive the same treatment as whites. Rustin knew the occasion was too ripe with promise to squander on symbolic gestures. The march would still officially be for "jobs and freedom," but with a much greater emphasis on the latter.

Even with Rustin's willingness to adjust his goals, it was not clear what his role in the march would be. Representatives of the participating organizations met for a planning session at New York City's Roosevelt Hotel on July 2. Randolph attended, along with the leaders of the five major civil rights groups: Wilkins of the NAACP, Young of the Urban League, King of SCLC, SNCC's John Lewis, and CORE's James Farmer. Each member of what became known as the Big Six would be allotted four minutes of speaking time at a rally on the Lincoln Memorial steps, which was scheduled for Wednesday, August 28. The leaders then turned to the question of who would organize the march. Randolph suggested Rustin, but Wilkins immediately objected. He insisted that they had enough to worry about without taking on a draft resister and ex-Communist, not to mention a homosexual with a "record." None of the other leaders rose to defend Rustin except Farmer, who went back twenty years with him to their time in the pacifist movement, and Randolph. King was noncommittal. Wilkins remained adamant. Finally, Randolph, the oldest and most respected man in the room, resorted to subterfuge to get what he wanted. After the group unanimously chose him as the march director, he said he wished to appoint an assistant: Bayard Rustin. An exasperated Wilkins threw up his hands, forced to acquiesce. Rustin was thus launched on the journey of his life.

Randolph quickly made it clear that he intended to be the march's director in name only. His deputy would be responsible for strategy, organization, and logistics. Rustin had his work cut out for him. The march was only eight weeks away. But he had spent most of his career as an activist preparing for this assignment, performing all the small duties in smaller venues that would serve him well when larger opportunities arose. "I'll study and get ready," Lincoln

Rustin with Martin Luther King, Jr. Source: Corbis.

once said, "and then the chance will come."[2] Rustin was ready when his chance came because he was familiar with the nuts and bolts of political protest in ways most civil rights leaders were not. He knew from experience how to publicize a demonstration, how to transport people there, how to feed them, where to set up a speaker's platform, how to assemble a sound system, and how to clean up afterward. Now he had the chance to employ those skills on a national stage.

He quickly moved into action. A sympathetic church allowed him to use a brownstone it owned on 130th Street in Harlem as the march's headquarters. Rustin filled it with desks, telephones, mimeograph machines, and assistants borrowed from participating organizations. He began to broaden the march's base to include labor and church groups. Although the American Federation of Labor and Congress of Industrial Organizations (AFL-CIO), the nation's largest labor association, declined to offer its official backing, it permitted its member unions to provide support. The United Auto Workers (UAW) weighed in with substantial financial assistance. UAW President Walter Reuther had a background in socialism and a strong commitment to civil rights causes. He gave enough money to the march to be invited to join its inner sanctum and was permitted to speak along with the other leaders at the Lincoln Memorial on August 28.

Reuther, in fact, may have typified the Northern white liberal supporter of the march. To him, its aims were simple matters of morality and justice. The existence of Jim Crow was an outrage in a nation that ostensibly promised all its citizens equal protection of the laws. That African Americans could not vote in the South was also shameful; the Fifteenth Amendment had been part of the Constitution for almost a century. Reuther supported Kennedy's civil rights bill because he believed that the white South had to change. And, of course, it did. But Reuther was able to make this demand almost reflexively because it concerned the South and not his own region. African Americans could eat at any restaurant in Detroit they could afford. There were no legally segregated swimming pools or water fountains. And not only could blacks vote in the Motor City, but they constituted a powerful political bloc that no local office seeker could ignore. Blacks in the North already possessed what the civil rights bill would guarantee in the South.

Reuther and other Northern liberals, then, could support the march as a matter of conscience and principle because it fixed the locus of injustice in another community. White Southerners needed to change their ways. White Northerners needed only to continue what they were already doing. The march allowed its Northern supporters the luxury of a moral superiority that Southern whites viewed as smug and hypocritical. After all, the North itself was filled with racial inequities. Restaurants in Northern cities might be open to blacks, but they often lacked the funds to patronize them. The average black worker earned only a fraction of his white counterpart. And while racism was not always obvious, as it was in the South, it still existed in more subtle forms. It was manifested in every dead-end job an African American was forced to accept, in every slum neighborhood that represented his only choice for housing, and in every substandard school his child had to attend. Northerners might acknowledge the existence of inequality in their own backyards, but it was tempting to turn away and instead focus on the South. When offered what amounted to a pass from historical responsibility at the March on Washington, Northern liberals like Reuther did not hesitate to avail themselves of it.

Rustin presided over the march organizing process during July and August like a maestro. Calm and collected amid the chaos of the brownstone on 130th Street, smoking constantly, issuing orders with clipped authority, he was in his element. He left nothing to chance. "If you want to organize anything," Rustin once said, "assume that everybody is absolutely stupid. And assume yourself that you are stupid."[3] He employed the membership resources of the NAACP and his own field operatives to spread word about the march in black communities across the country. He made sure transportation to the capital on the day of the march would be smooth and efficient, arranging for buses to park where they could conveniently discharge and pick up demonstrators. He trained a force of internal security marshals from the ranks of black police officers to insulate the marchers from confrontations with white law enforcement. He provided for nonperishable food in anticipation of the Washington summer heat. He personally approved the language on the signs to be carried by the demonstrators to ensure that the messages of racial equality, integration, and support for the civil rights bill would not be obscured. He put together a squad of cleaners to swoop in at the conclusion of the march so the demonstration area would be left pristine. He even ordered portable toilets to be placed alongside the Mall in order to maintain public decency. Thinking like a person who was "stupid," Rustin used his decades of organizing experience to anticipate contingencies that would have escaped the notice of his less worldly colleagues.

Rustin was obsessed with the details of the march for another reason. The prospect of thousands of African Americans descending on the city had thrown official Washington, D.C., into a panic. Stereotypes of disorderly, disruptive, and uncontrollable blacks abounded in white America in 1963, and Rustin was determined to disprove them. The demeanor of the march would be as important as its content. If Rustin could keep the largest public gathering of African Americans in the nation's history peaceful and orderly, it would not only confirm the efficacy of nonviolent protest as a political instrument, but also challenge racial attitudes that had been entrenched for centuries. Racial conservatives in the United States had historically argued that the "hearts and minds" of white Americans had to change before blacks could become fully vested citizens. An incident-free March on Washington could thus recast the national racial climate.

Rustin with Cleveland Robinson, chairman of administrative committee for March on Washington and placard announcing March on Washington, August 1963. Source: Library of Congress.

Rustin also knew that the president was skittish about the march. It had taken Kennedy two and a half years of his term in office to "come around" on civil rights. Until the events at Birmingham, he had treated the issue as an annoyance, an unwelcome diversion from the nation's struggle with the Soviet Union for global supremacy. His administration's support for the 1961 Freedom

Rides had been minimal. His use of federal power to integrate the Universities of Mississippi and Alabama in 1962 and 1963 was as much a demonstration of his executive authority as a commitment to racial justice. Once, when confronted by a group of African diplomats who had been refused service at a Maryland rest stop while driving from New York to Washington to meet with him, Kennedy advised them to avoid future problems by traveling by air instead. But having taken the step of introducing a potentially groundbreaking piece of civil rights legislation, he now faced the daunting task of steering it through a Congress presided over by Southern committee chairmen and susceptible to Southern-inspired filibusters. In these circumstances, any untoward event or revelation could derail the bill.

Kennedy was thus concerned about the impact of the march on congressional sensibilities. The potential dangers were twofold. Even the hint of violence could alienate legislators who associated the civil rights movement with "disorder." These included Republicans whose votes would be needed to defeat a filibuster. Senate Minority Leader Everett Dirksen of Illinois and House Minority Leader Charles Halleck of Indiana were both traditional Republicans with conservative cultural sensibilities. They viewed King as a troublemaker whose politics and methods lay outside the American mainstream. Kennedy ran the risk of losing them and the civil rights bill if the march exhibited any appearance of impropriety.

Kennedy also knew that the issue of Communist involvement hung over the march. Although a vigorous Cold Warrior himself, Kennedy feared the "soft on communism" label that Republicans had wielded against liberal Democrats since the heyday of Joseph McCarthy. "Guilt by association" could taint even a president, and if the Kennedy administration were to be linked to left-wing figures in the civil rights movement, the political consequences would be dire. The FBI had told the president about Stanley Levison's Communist ties, as well as those of another King confidante, Jack O'Dell. At a White House meeting, Kennedy told the SCLC leader to distance himself from them. King acceded, at least for the time being.

Kennedy's discomfort with the march reflected a contemporary political culture in which even peaceful civil rights demonstrations were viewed as destabilizing and any tenuous connection with communism considered illegitimate. Rustin knew he had to allay the president's concerns. He succeeded in doing so by channeling the march's momentum toward the center of that political culture. The Big Six of African American leaders was expanded to comprise a Big Ten. Each of the four additions—Reuther, plus representatives of the Protestant, Catholic, and Jewish clergy—was white. The archbishop of Washington, Patrick Cardinal O'Boyle, was recruited to participate in the march's opening ceremony. Rustin planned to have the Big Ten spend the morning of the march meeting with congressional leaders and visit with the president in the Oval Office in the late afternoon. He wanted the emphasis of the entire day to be on shared values and inclusion. Rustin wanted whites to understand that African Americans wished to join them as national citizens, and that they cherished the historic expressions of that citizenship—the Declaration of Independence, the Constitution, the Gettysburg Address—as much as whites. Rustin envisioned the march as a medium through which the civil rights movement could reach the heart of white America.

There was, of course, one part of white America that refused to be moved, and it struck back with a vengeance against both the march and its chief organizer. On August 2 and again on August 7 and 13, Senator Strom Thurmond of South Carolina, one of the nation's most prominent defenders of Jim Crow, denounced Rustin from the floor of Congress. He introduced portions of Rustin's FBI history into the Congressional Record, including his Communist background and record of arrests for civil disobedience, draft resistance, and public indecency. Thurmond intended this last item to be most damaging of all. He hoped that it would destroy the march's credibility by forcing Rustin's departure just before it was to take place.

Rustin with plans for route of March on Washington, August 1963. Source: AP/Wide World Photos.

Under different circumstances, he might have succeeded. But Randolph and Wilkins knew that without Rustin, there was no march. They leapt to his defense, both in public and behind the scenes, planting stories extolling Rustin's high ethical standards and commitment to nonviolence in the national media. They met with march supporters to head off defections. Randolph used the immense personal respect he had generated during a half century of activism to shield Rustin. He deflected the issue of the 1953 Pasadena arrest with the deftness of a seasoned political operator, issuing a statement that referred obliquely to the incident, and then questioned Thurmond's motives in reviving it. This was enough for a Northern white constituency familiar with the brutalities of Jim Crow. Southern politicians who countenanced the use of fire hoses and German shepherds on children in Birmingham were hardly in a position to act as protectors of decency and morality. The controversy soon died down, a sign of the nation's shifting sexual mores as well as Rustin's value to the march.

As August 28 drew nearer, Rustin turned to the entertainment world for assistance. By the 1960s, national culture was increasingly grounded in media and celebrity, and as a veteran promoter of movements and causes, Rustin understood what "sold." He worked with actor/singer Harry Belafonte to organize a contingent of stars to publicize the march to a mass audience. The presence of Belafonte, along with notables such as Paul Newman, Marlon Brando, and Burt Lancaster, would connect the march's politics to popular culture and give it a resonance far beyond that of a more prosaic demonstration or rally. Rustin was creating an event, a "happening." And, in a final stroke of marketing genius, he scheduled King to be the last speaker on August 28, a choice that would have historic consequences.

By the week of the march, Rustin had assembled an interracial coalition of civil rights activists, labor leaders, clergy, entertainment figures, Democratic Party officials, and concerned citizens in support of the Kennedy civil rights bill. Although the march's agenda no longer emphasized economic justice, it was still expansive enough to presage a revolution in American race relations. Rustin had taken the march into the realm of spectacle and the issue of civil rights into the American popular imagination. In the future, he would attempt to reassemble the alliance of August 28, 1963, convinced that it held the key to his egalitarian dream. But just as elements of his dream had crashed against each other during his time in the shadows, so they would as he moved toward the American mainstream.

The snares of coalition politics were made manifest even before the march had begun. The speech SNCC's John Lewis had prepared for the rally angered some of its more conservative participants, including Cardinal O'Boyle, who refused to appear unless its language was softened. Lewis represented the most militant of the major civil rights groups. SNCC's field workers were waging a grassroots voter registration drive in the South that was eliciting a violent counterreaction. Lewis arrived in Washington on August 26, two days before the march, in a less than conciliatory mood. His speech was full of angry rhetoric. It lambasted the civil rights bill as "too little, and too late." It called for a nonviolent march through the South reminiscent of General William T. Sherman's bloody Civil War rampage, one that would "burn Jim Crow to the ground." Lewis threatened to "fragment the South into a thousand pieces and put them back together in the image of democracy." His speech also employed a word with which Rustin, at least, was familiar: "revolution."[4] This was too much for Cardinal O'Boyle, as well as for Wilkins and Young. Randolph, while defending the use of the word, was also disturbed by Lewis's overall tone.

Rustin's position was more ambiguous. Twenty years earlier, he would have endorsed this speech, and perhaps even written it himself. But the controversy over the Lewis draft symbolized the distance between where Rustin had been and where he was going, between purity and pragmatism. Rustin may have agreed on an emotional level with much of what Lewis had written, but the stakes were now too high. The march itself was in danger. By August 27, with only twenty-four hours to go, it had assumed a singular place in his mind and heart. The March on Washington had become the defining work of his life, and he could not afford to let it go, even over a matter of principle. It was not everything he wanted, but it represented what was possible at the moment. And if he could maintain the coalition he had built for the march, he might yet realize his dreams. So while Lewis's rhetoric was compelling, Rustin knew what had to be done. He arranged a meeting at which he and the march leaders asked Lewis to moderate his language. Lewis and the SNCC representatives were furious. Never entirely comfortable with the aims of the march in the first place, they initially refused to budge. For his efforts at compromise, Rustin was lambasted as a "sellout," not the last time he would hear this epithet. Negotiations continued that night and into the day of the march itself. It took a personal plea from Randolph to convince Lewis to give in, and a Rustin aide rewrote his words only moments before he was to deliver them.

This disharmony, however, lay beneath the surface. What America saw on August 28, 1963, was, thanks largely to Rustin, a public display of unity and singleness of purpose unmatched in the history of the American civil rights movement. Early in the morning, the first demonstrators began to trickle in. Washington, D.C., officials, still expecting violence, had prepared accordingly. Most government workers stayed home, sales of alcoholic beverages in the city were prohibited, and local military were in readiness. Rustin positioned himself on the Mall, talking to the media and watching the fruits of his meticulous planning unfold.

Rustin briefing marshals before March on Washington. Source: Corbis.

The day was sunny and warm. There was some humidity, but the city was not the blast furnace it often resembles in August. By 9:30 A.M., some 25,000 marchers had assembled at the Washington Monument, a half mile down the Mall from the Lincoln Memorial, where the speeches would be delivered. By 10 A.M., the number had risen to 40,000; by 11 A.M., 90,000; and by noon, 200,000. The crowd would eventually total 250,000, about one quarter of it white. After their morning meetings on Capitol Hill, the March leaders returned to the Washington Monument, where the gathering demonstrators had been entertained by folksingers Joan Baez; Bob Dylan; Peter, Paul, and Mary; and Rustin's old musical colleague Josh White. Rustin's plan was to have the organization heads lead the procession down the Mall to the Lincoln Memorial, but near midday the rank-and-file could wait no longer and spontaneously marched there themselves. King, Randolph, and the others were forced to wedge their way into the crowd as it streamed forward.

The proceedings on the Lincoln Memorial steps featured an announcement by Wilkins that was tinged with irony. W. E. B. Du Bois had struggled most of his life to live as both an American and an African American. He had inspired Rustin's own dreams, and by extension, those of the March on Washington itself. But by the 1950s, Du Bois was a Marxist hounded by the government. He gave up on this struggle and on the United States, moving to Ghana. He died there on August 27, the day before the march.

Rustin was probably too busy to ponder the significance of this news. The issue of Lewis's speech remained unresolved, at least in the minds of angry SNCC activists. Negotiations over his language continued in a small room in the basement of the Lincoln Memorial. By this time Rustin had moved past ideology. He was willing to do almost anything to preserve the march's fragile unity. But even the ostensibly "toned down" version Lewis gave contained intimations of future discord within both the civil rights movement and the American left generally, which would have profound implications for Rustin's own career.

When Lewis excoriated the "immoral compromises" of contemporary American politics, he was referring primarily to mainstream white politicians, but also to the civil rights leaders who dealt with them.[5] Lewis and his SNCC colleagues prided themselves on their popular roots and moral authenticity. They were not "boardroom" or "Oval Office" figures like Wilkins, Young, or even King. Indeed, their work for Southern voting rights notwithstanding, they were suspicious of the "compromises" associated with electoral politics. A younger Rustin would have shared Lewis's unwillingness to join in the give-and-take of traditional political negotiation. But his new agenda required just these types of adjustments and accommodations. What a Catholic archbishop thought about the tenor of the march did not matter to Lewis, but it now did to Rustin. While SNCC activists had been picketing Kennedy's Justice Department the night before the march, Rustin was trying desperately to keep it from unraveling. His had been among the voices urging moderation on Lewis. The controversy over the Lewis speech marked the beginning of a rift between Rustin and grassroots civil rights leaders that would widen over the course of the decade, as what Rustin viewed as realism came to be interpreted by others as a sellout to white vested interests.

The remainder of the afternoon proceeded more harmoniously. There was a festival-like atmosphere in the interracial crowd and no major disturbances. The 250,000 participants comprised the largest mass political gathering in U.S. history. Thanks to the demonstrators' earlier-than-anticipated push down the Mall to the Lincoln Memorial, the rally stayed roughly on schedule. A potential source of embarrassment was avoided when Malcolm X, who had come to ridicule what he sardonically referred to as the "Farce on Washington," chose to stay away from the march area itself. Millions across America watched live CBS coverage, with the two other major networks breaking in for King's speech. And it was King for whom the crowd waited. Along with Lewis, each Big Ten member (except CORE's Farmer, who was serving a jail sentence in Louisiana) took his turn on the podium. Mahalia Jackson, the famous gospel singer, delivered emotional renderings of spirituals. Finally, at 3:30, Randolph walked to the microphone and introduced the day's last speaker, Martin Luther King, Jr., as "the moral leader of our nation."[6] To loud cheers, King stepped forward and stood framed by the columns of the Lincoln Memorial and the seated figure of the sixteenth president.

King delivered the greatest speech in the history of American race relations. His concluding sentences, unscheduled and spoken from memory after Jackson blurted out, "tell 'em about the dream, Martin," immortalized him and what became known in the national imagination as the "I Have a Dream" address.[7] The drama of the occasion, the eloquence of his delivery, and his huge audience—including many white Americans who were hearing him for the first time—ensured that his words would resonate long after King left the platform, and long after his death.

The speech was a triumph both as a political and religious document. King invoked the Declaration of Independence, the Constitution, the Emancipation Proclamation, and even the song "My Country 'Tis of Thee" to show that his dream was "deeply rooted in the American dream," and that blacks as well as whites were heirs to the nation's democratic and egalitarian heritage.[8] The cause of civil rights was America's cause and an affirmation of its political traditions. King situated the civil rights movement at the heart of the struggle to achieve America's central values—equality and freedom.

He combined this vision of political redemption with a spiritual one. Masterfully linking the religious and the secular, King argued that the Bible's egalitarian, liberating prophecies could only be fulfilled in the United States. America was a uniquely blessed nation, the instrument of God's sacred plan for all mankind. By living up to their political ideals, Americans—all of them—would be obeying God's will and attaining spiritual perfection. Not since Lincoln's 1865 Second Inaugural Address, which identified slavery as a biblical sin and the bloody Civil War as its penitence, had an American orator so powerfully expressed the connection between the nation's values and its soul.

But how to define those values? What did "equality" and "freedom" mean in America? King used these words throughout the "I Have a Dream" speech, but like Lincoln before him, he left much unsaid. It was left to King's audience—which, thanks to television, comprised many more whites than blacks—to give his language meaning. For example, King mentioned poverty only once in his speech. He referred to it briefly as he began ("the Negro lives on a lonely island of poverty"), but did not return to it again.[9] His address was otherwise devoid of explicit demands for economic equality. Instead, King situated freedom and equality within a legal/political framework that shifted the primary burden of change to the South and made the realization of his "dream" directly contingent on the passage of the Kennedy civil rights bill. The examples King offered of freedoms denied—segregated lodging, "whites only" signs in public facilities, police brutality, and disenfranchisement—were legal, not economic. Change the law, and change it in the South, King appeared to imply, and his visions of "equality" and "freedom" would come to pass.

King's Northern white listeners were deeply moved by his words, especially those that became the most widely quoted in the speech and most closely associated with him historically: "I have a dream that my four little children will one day live in a nation where they will not be judged by the color of their skin but by the content of their character."[10] King's rhetorical embrace of a race-blind ideal seemed to affirm the practices of the North, where there was no legalized segregation, where blacks could vote, and where—or so Northern whites believed—men and women were already judged on their character. King, in their view, was merely giving his blessing to what they were doing on their own. As long as King's focus was on law and politics and not on economics and poverty, Northern whites could assume that he believed "freedom" and "equality" would be achieved in the United States at little or no cost to them through the passage of legislation that they generally supported, and that responsibility for the nation's racial injustices lay elsewhere. Thus, like Rustin, King accepted the constrained political parameters of the march. Any meaningful discussion of economic injustice in America would have required him to speak of redistribution of resources, with benefits to be transferred from whites to blacks. This would not only have contradicted his "content of their character" phraseology, but the language of the address as a whole.

The "I Have a Dream" speech, an oration for the ages, nonetheless begged questions that King and Rustin knew white Americans were not ready to address.

In the short term, this was probably wise. The success of the march depended to a great degree on white support. But the "I Have a Dream" speech led much of King's white Northern constituency to conclude that the goals of freedom and equality demanded no sacrifices from them. In time this would cause deep divisions in the civil rights alliance that Rustin had worked so hard to construct. By 1968, as King called for a massive attack on poverty in the form of a Poor People's Campaign, which was openly redistributionist, many Northern whites who had cheered the "I Have a Dream" speech at the March on Washington abandoned him. Both King and Rustin would face a bitter reckoning born of the compromises and calculated omissions of the march itself.

But this lay in the future as King concluded his speech to an explosive interracial ovation. After Randolph recapitulated the march's ongoing objectives for the audience, it was the chief organizer's turn. Stepping forward, arms aloft, Rustin stood in triumph and took in the appreciation of a quarter of a million people. The day belonged to him as much as it did to King. A decade earlier, Rustin had been unemployed and shunned, a convicted "sex offender" fresh out of jail. Now thousands were cheering him. He would never return to the shadows, not after this day. And perhaps, his dream for America might yet come true. Looking out over a sea of smiling faces, black and white, anything seemed possible.

Notes

1. Clayborne Carson, et al., eds., *Eyes on the Prize: America's Civil Rights Years* (New York: Penguin, 1987), p. 120.

2. Gene Griessman, *The Words Lincoln Lived By* (New York: Simon & Schuster, 1997), p. 65.

3. Quoted in Taylor Branch, *Parting the Waters: America in the King Years, 1954–63* (New York: Simon & Schuster, 1988), p. 873.

4. Carson, et al., *Eyes on the Prize*, pp. 122, 123.

5. A. Philip Randolph, et al., *Speeches by the Leaders: The March on Washington for Jobs and Freedom, August 28, 1963* (New York: NAACP, 1963).

6. Quoted in Branch, *Parting the Waters*, p. 881.

7. Quoted in Branch, *Parting the Waters*, p. 882.

8. Clayborne Carson and Kris Shepard, eds., *A Call to Conscience: The Landmark Speeches of Dr. Martin Luther King, Jr.* (New York: Warner Books, 2001), pp. 81, 82, 85, 86.

9. Carson and Shepard, *A Call to Conscience*, p. 81.

10. Carson and Shepard, *A Call to Conscience*, p. 85.

~

CHAPTER FOUR

Coalition Politics and Its Limits, 1963–1969

After the grateful applause of the March on Washington audience died down, Rustin asked the crowd to repeat an oath to return to communities across the nation and work at the grassroots level for jobs and freedom. As the happy marchers drifted away, Rustin, efficient to the last, deployed teams to scour the Mall for debris. When they completed their work, the area was immaculate. Rustin attended to final details as King, Randolph, Wilkins, and the other march leaders met with Kennedy at the White House. With evident relief, the president praised the day's nonviolent spirit. Kennedy's misgivings had been unjustified. His civil rights bill was in much better condition than it had been that morning.

Back on the Mall, Rustin let the wonder of the day's events sink in. There was much to ponder. The civil rights movement was now a national movement—King's speech had seen to that. Hundreds of thousands of black and white Americans had proved by example that nonviolence was a powerful moral force and an instrument of profound social change. And the coalition that had made the march a success—civil rights organizations, labor unions, organized religion, and Democratic Party leaders—had transformative potential that dwarfed that of the small socialist and peace groups through which Rustin had worked during the past two decades. This coalition had touched millions of consciences at the march, but it could do much more. It could pass the civil rights bill. It could enfranchise Southern blacks. It could provide the political muscle for an attack on poverty that went far beyond what President Kennedy was then mulling, one that featured a massive program of social expenditures guaranteeing every American a job, a living income, a good education, adequate housing, and proper medical care. This coalition could negotiate the issue of economic justice in the

United States in a way that would unite Americans of all races. It could thus move beyond the equality under the law that had been the focus of the march and on to the economic equality that was the true mark of a democratic society: Racial justice. Economic justice. If the March on Washington coalition could hold together, August 28, 1963, might have just been the beginning.

Rustin spent the rest of his life pursuing his American dream through the march's alliances. But the success of that day came to haunt him. Rustin learned that the triumphant hours on the Mall had been only a brief moment of unity and agreement. The stresses of the 1960s would splinter the elements of the march's coalition and send them careening in different directions. The war in Vietnam broke off some parts. The civil rights movement's retreat from integrationism fissured others. But perhaps most disappointing of all to Rustin was the nation's failure to embrace the dream of economic justice that had appeared so promising at the March on Washington. Rustin made many sacrifices for this dream. But for all his efforts, a viable constituency for economic democracy in America—for his dream of a job, income, education, housing, and health care for every citizen—did not materialize.

It has been said that Americans integrate by class as reluctantly as they do by race, and the failure of Rustin's democratic socialist agenda to gain traction even after the unity and purpose of the March on Washington may offer a real-life illustration of this adage. Certainly this was the case among white Americans, whose disillusionment with Lyndon Johnson's War on Poverty drove them rightward economically in the late 1960s and 1970s. But it also may have been true of African Americans, especially those representing the more militant wing of the civil rights movement, who saw in Rustin's call for a cross-race coalition of the poor and working class based on nonviolence and integrationism the continuation of white domination by less direct means. Ultimately, Rustin was not able to convince enough Americans of either race that an "equal" nation was one without substantial class distinctions.

The March on Washington made Rustin a political celebrity. He was now a national media figure, a fixture on the airwaves, in newspapers and magazines, and on the lecture circuit. He remained so for the rest of his life. But for all his newfound importance, he could not achieve his agenda. The years following the March on Washington offered a harsh lesson on the differences between prominence and influence, as well as on the dangerous entanglements of race and class in the United States. At the end of the 1960s, the elements of his dream would collide a final time, in the cruelest way imaginable.

Rustin's immediate goal after the march was the preservation of its organizational structure, much as Randolph had done in 1941 after the cancellation of his Washington demonstration for fair employment practices. The September 15 bombing of a Birmingham church, which killed four African American girls, lent Rustin's project a heightened degree of urgency. Despite the widespread outrage in the civil rights community over the murders, however, there was little sentiment for retaining a March on Washington administrative apparatus. A continuing March on Washington organization headed by Rustin would offer him a platform from which to eclipse the less personable Roy Wilkins, as well as the Urban League's Whitney Young and CORE's James Farmer. With no support from within the civil rights movement and no independent access to funds, the March on Washington organization quietly disbanded. If Rustin was to have a permanent base of operations, he would have to find it elsewhere.

Early in 1964 Rustin thought he had located such a home in the SCLC, when the group offered him a position in New York. Once again, however, controversy intervened. This time, it involved Rustin's politics and not his sexuality. In February, Rustin and Muste paid a visit to the Soviet United Nations mission in New York to confer with a peace group. The FBI had stepped up its surveillance in the wake of Rustin's March on Washington–inspired notoriety, and thanks to a telephone wiretap, it knew of his itinerary. FBI director J. Edgar Hoover made sure newspaper reporters were waiting for Rustin when he arrived at the mission. Predictably, the stories that appeared the next day portrayed him as a dupe of the "reds." Rustin's anti-Communist credentials were strong and of long vintage, and it was clear that he was guilty of little more than a lapse in judgment. But once again, he was "too hot to handle," and SCLC could not afford to support him in an atmosphere of continued Cold War tension. It quietly dropped Rustin from consideration. Even his position with the War Resisters League had become tenuous. Rustin had spent as much time on leave from the group as he had running it during the past few years, as the focus of his activism shifted toward civil rights. The March on Washington may have made him into a political celebrity, but professionally Rustin was still adrift.

There was also the practical issue of making a living. As Rustin grew older, he developed an affinity for fine objects, including artwork and antiques. He returned from trips abroad laden with such items and visited galleries and stores in New York whenever his schedule permitted. Although Rustin was by no means a spendthrift, he required an income appropriate to his lifestyle. Even committed radicals crave some measure of stability, and years of precarious finances had taken their toll.

By 1964 Rustin was moving toward the center both politically and personally. The incident at the Soviet United Nations mission was the last time he allowed himself to be caught in a situation that compromised him in the eyes of mainstream labor and Democratic Party leaders. Rustin continued to seek the counsel of Muste and Randolph and respect their opinions. But the influence of figures such as Lyndon Johnson, Senator Hubert Humphrey, and labor leaders George Meany and Walter Reuther on his outlook was growing, and his politics was bending toward theirs. Over the next few years, Rustin's growing sense of political pragmatism and his desire for personal security led him toward positions that his colleagues in the peace and civil rights movements in the 1940s and 1950s would not have recognized.

Early in 1964 Rustin attempted to employ the alliance of African Americans, white liberals, unionists, and church members who had been so potent at the March on Washington in a campaign to integrate the public schools of New York City. The city's education system was less racially integrated in 1964 than it had been when the *Brown* decision was issued a decade earlier. A combination of residential segregation in the city's neighborhoods and white parent resistance to busing initiatives had created deeply divided educational environments for black and white schoolchildren. There were also wide, racialized disparities in teacher quality, facilities, supplies, and test score levels, creating an achievement gap that Rustin feared would affect the fabric of city life for generations.

Local chapters of the NAACP and CORE were pressing the cause of school integration in New York, and Rustin joined with them. But there were also grassroots educational activists already in place, and their work intrigued Rustin. They had been fighting for integration, largely outside the city's political power structure, since the *Brown* decision. Their leader, Milton Galamison, a Brooklyn African American minister, had used his and other congregations to build an interracial, neighborhood-based advocacy network to lobby board of education officials, file lawsuits, and stage demonstrations and sit-ins across the city. When Galamison asked Rustin to coordinate a pro-integration boycott of the New York public schools planned for February 3, 1964, he eagerly accepted.

Rustin threw himself into preparations for the boycott in a manner reminiscent of his work the previous summer on the March on Washington. Once again, he left nothing to chance. Although the March on Washington had required him to bring thousands of people to one location, his task now was to disperse protesters all over the city. He used Galamison's community organizations to staff picket lines at hundreds of schools, and set up alternative or "freedom" schools, at which boycotting students would be taught for the day. Rustin envisioned the freedom schools as both an answer to boycott critics who would decry the loss of a day's instruction, and a way to expose city youth to nonviolent direct action as a strategy and philosophy. Rustin knew that the cooperation of the union representing New York public schoolteachers, the United Federation of Teachers (UFT), would be crucial to the success of his freedom school plan. Rustin was also counting on organized labor to anchor the movement for political, social, and economic equality in the United States, which he envisioned as the March on Washington's ongoing legacy. Rustin urged the UFT leadership to publicly support the boycott and ask its members to stay out of their classrooms on February 3.

But the union had concerns of its own. The UFT was a relatively young organization. Founded in 1960, it was newly certified as the exclusive bargaining agent for the city's teachers. The UFT had enthusiastically supported the March on Washington. Its members were staunch racial liberals who donated generously to the SCLC and were aligned politically with civil rights supporters in the Democratic Party. But New York State law prohibited public employee strikes and punished strikers with jail sentences and fines. To Rustin's disappointment, UFT officials placed the union's well-being above the cause of racial justice. Union President Albert Shanker advised teachers to take February 3 as a sick or personal day, thus enabling them to avoid a direct confrontation with state and city authorities. This was not the clear statement Rustin wanted. The union's half measure damaged the boycott in an immediate sense, since students would be more inclined to stay away from school if their teachers announced they would also do so. It also illustrated the tensions that lay at the intersection of labor and civil rights in the United States, which would entrap Rustin later in the decade.

The boycott was not a success. Almost half of the city's pupils stayed out of school on February 3, but Rustin had hoped for a much higher percentage. He was able to organize picketing and freedom schools in most areas. A rally at city hall in the afternoon drew 2,500 protesters. Coverage in the local media was extensive, but participation rates varied sharply by race. White student support for the boycott was only a quarter of that among blacks and Hispanics.[1] The overwhelmingly white UFT membership treated February 3 like any other school day. Only 8 percent were absent, about as many as would normally be out.[2]

Rustin's logistical work was a model of preparation and order, as it had been at the March on Washington. But he did not achieve his goal, and the city's schools remained segregated. The boycott was the first of what would be many failed attempts to recapture the march's shared sense of purpose. The New York school boycott showed that those upon whom Rustin was staking his American dream—poor and working-class blacks, white unionists, liberals, church members—could not be relied on to define "equality" and "freedom" in the same ways. Did the well-being of a labor union outweigh the cause of public school integration? Did class issues outweigh those related to race? During the New York school boycott, Rustin was again caught between the competing demands of labor and civil rights. The boycott's inconclusive result—impressive turnout, positive media coverage, but no appreciable effect on the racial distribution of students in the public schools—postponed a final reckoning with the consequences of these clashing imperatives.

Rustin rationalized the UFT's tepid response to the boycott as a necessary act of self-preservation. The intentions of the union's leaders and members, he believed,

Rustin (far left) at a summit conference on civil rights, with (from left) Jack Greenberg, NAACP Educational & Legal Defense Fund; Whitney Young, National Urban League; James Farmer, CORE; Roy Wilkins, NAACP; Martin Luther King Jr., SCLC; John Lewis, SNCC; and A. Philip Randolph, Brotherhood of Sleeping Car Porters, New York, NY, July 1964. Source: AP/Wide World Photos.

were good. White unionists and African Americans were natural allies, and if the UFT had not faced a plausible threat of retaliation from state authorities, it would have joined him. But Rustin's views may have been colored by wishful thinking. He had staked so much of his dream on the race-labor alliance that he could not bring himself to admit that there might have been another explanation for the behavior of the UFT leadership. School integration was important to Shanker and other union officials, but when it conflicted with what was to them an even more important goal—the security of the union—their choice was clear. For the time being, Rustin could straddle both sides of the civil rights–labor rights divide, and, indeed, maintain that it did not even exist. But this uneasy equilibrium would not survive for long. The 1964 school boycott was a prelude to more difficult times to come.

There was happier news on the national political front. On July 2, 1964, after a lengthy struggle in Congress, President Lyndon Johnson, who had succeeded the assassinated Kennedy the previous November, signed the Civil Rights Act. The new law prohibited all forms of public accommodation discrimination and provided for equal employment opportunity. The passage of what had originated as Kennedy's civil rights bill achieved the immediate objective of the March on Washington. The Southern Jim Crow system was now itself illegal. Almost a century after it was ratified, the Fourteenth Amendment's promise of equal protection of the laws to all citizens regardless of color was finally a reality. Rustin could take pride in the role he had played in this victory. King may have been the figure most associated with the law in the public's mind, but Rustin knew that had it not been for his counsel at Montgomery and his planning for the March on Washington, the "King" acclaimed by the nation and world would not exist. And without a King to drive events, another generation might have passed before Jim Crow finally came to an end.

Rustin had also come to believe in the president who had guided the Civil Rights Act into law. Lyndon Johnson was a Southerner with a deep sense of racial justice. He knew that only through the passage of strong civil rights legislation could his region finally put to rest the wounds of the Civil War. Under Jim Crow, the South had remained an economic backwater for almost a century. Blacks and whites alike lived there in poverty and despair. Only by ending the era of white supremacy could the South break out of its isolation and open up to the rest of the United States. It could become a place of opportunity, with a healthy economy that would attract the talented and educated of all races. Johnson thus viewed the Civil Rights Act as imperative. He pushed it though both houses of Congress with ruthless political skill.

Rustin was impressed. Here was a special president, sensitive to the needs of African Americans, with the ability to get laws passed that were generations overdue. The Civil Rights Act might have been the start of a legislative revolution.

Johnson seemed to share Rustin's passion for economic justice as well. Like Rustin, the president wanted every American to have a job, an income, adequate medical care, and decent housing. Johnson had launched the War on Poverty through the Economic Opportunity Act, which Congress passed in August 1964.

The War on Poverty was a multipronged effort to assist the disadvantaged Americans for whom Rustin had been fighting his entire career. LBJ's antipoverty program, it was true, did not go as far as Rustin wished. It concentrated primarily on training and education for employment in an expanding American economy, and not on direct assistance to those in need. Johnson had considered embarking on a guaranteed minimum income and jobs program, but discarded the idea, fearing that it would be too expensive and stifle individual initiative. But his War on Poverty did establish the principle that the federal government was responsible for the economic well-being of every American, an idea that was at the heart of Rustin's own philosophy. In Rustin's mind, the War on Poverty was a first step toward his own dream. It could expand over time to include Rustin's more ambitious agenda if enough Americans organized through the vehicle of the Democratic Party. By the summer of 1964, Rustin's stake in the party and in Johnson was enormous. He viewed the Johnson administration as ripe with possibility. The president's reelection, he now argued, was imperative.

Rustin proved his loyalty to Johnson in August 1964 at the Democratic National Convention in Atlantic City, New Jersey, during SNCC's campaign to desegregate the lily-white Mississippi state Democratic Party. Earlier that year, SNCC, with Rustin's assistance, had organized the "Freedom Summer" voter registration drive in that state. Rustin was the drive's Northern point man, raising money and generating publicity. He also conducted workshops on nonviolent social change for white Northern student volunteers who relocated south to work with local SNCC activists. The volunteers encountered fierce opposition from the defenders of Jim Crow in Mississippi. Uncooperative voter registrars, who disqualified potential black voters on any pretext, were the most visible manifestations of the system. But there was also a violent underside, composed of local "law enforcement" officials and Ku Klux Klan vigilantes, who would stop at nothing to protect their "way of life." In June, as if to emphasize this point, three Freedom Summer participants—two white Northerners and a Southern black—were murdered by a white deputy sheriff and his accomplices. Their bodies were not found until August.

Rustin and SNCC leaders knew that the white stranglehold on what was known as the "regular" Mississippi Democratic Party had to be broken. They decided to create a competing organization, composed almost completely of African Americans, which they named the Mississippi Freedom Democratic Party (MFDP). The MFDP would propose a delegate slate at the Democratic National Convention to replace the all-white delegation of the regular state party. Taking its case directly to the convention, the MFDP would dramatize the exclusion of African Americans from the political process in Mississippi and elsewhere in the South to Northern white liberals and the national Democratic Party. Surely, MFDP leaders believed, Johnson, who had made passage of the Civil Rights Act his top legislative priority, would insist on seating their delegates in place of the white regulars.

But Johnson had other ideas. Although committed to civil rights, he was first and foremost a pragmatic politician. He had worked his way up from rural Texas obscurity to the White House and viewed the upcoming Democratic convention as the pinnacle of his career. With his nomination unopposed, Johnson turned his attention to the issue of party unity, which the MFDP's campaign threatened to disrupt. The South had voted solidly Democratic for over a century. Despite the party's more liberal position on racial issues, the president still hoped to salvage much of the region in the general election against Republican Senator Barry Goldwater of Arizona, a conservative who had opposed the Civil Rights Act. If he could carry the South, Johnson's margin of victory might rival that of Franklin Roosevelt's in the landslide presidential election of 1936, in which FDR won 61 percent of the popular vote, 46 of 48 states, and 523 to 8 in the Electoral College.[3] Johnson was thus determined to keep the MFDP in the background.

When the convention opened in Atlantic City in late August, Rustin helped the MFDP apply to the party's credentials committee for recognition as Mississippi's official democratic delegation. One of the group's leaders, Fannie Lou Hamer, told the committee of the violent retribution she had suffered for attempting to register to vote. Her televised testimony was so graphic and dramatic that a nervous Johnson scheduled an announcement on a pretext in order to preempt her; the networks nonetheless replayed Hamer's appearance on videotape that night. Rustin pressed the MFDP's case to Democratic Party liberals and to labor leaders, including Minnesota Senator Hubert Humphrey and the United Auto Workers' Walter Reuther, who had been a strong supporter of the March on Washington. But Johnson ordered Reuther and Humphrey—who was about to become his vice presidential nominee—to put together a compromise. Rustin arranged a meeting between Humphrey, Reuther, and the MFDP leaders to hear the administration's offer. Johnson proposed that the delegate selection rules be revised to prohibit discrimination in future conventions. For the present, however, the segregated regular Mississippi delegation would be seated. As a consolation, MFDP would receive two at-large delegate seats.

MFDP leaders were bitterly disappointed. They considered the administration's plan a betrayal of a morally righteous cause. After all, who except the most hardened racist could describe an electoral system from which African Americans were excluded as "just"? Even Johnson understood that the system had to change. Why not change it immediately? Rustin too had hoped to recast the South's closed-off politics in one decisive blow at the 1964 convention. His work was a major reason the MFDP had come as far as it had. But Rustin also had ties to the president. He was caught between his desire to seat the MFDP delegation and his hopes of influencing the Johnson administration, between principle and pragmatism.

Rustin chose to be practical. He advised the MFDP to take what the president was offering. They deserved more, he said, but Johnson's version of real-world politics was not always fair. A morally superior position was not always a guarantee of success. Instead, Rustin argued, one built coalitions, achieved what was possible, and avoided burning bridges to those who could offer assistance. An opponent one day could be an ally the next. The MFDP was in effect being invited to become a Democratic Party "insider," a part of its power structure. In the future, African Americans and not white Southerners would wield influence in the party. But along with power would come a new responsibility to forgo the certainties of the protester for the accommodations of the politician. Only in this way, Rustin told the MFDP, could victories like the one at hand be won.

But MFDP members did not regard the compromise that Rustin urged upon them as a "victory." Their moral calculations were simple. The regular Mississippi delegates had been selected in a racially discriminatory manner. They did not deserve to be seated. That racists were being rewarded was an outrage. Promises of just treatment at later conventions did not sway the members of the MFDP. They wanted justice now. They angrily rejected the Johnson proposal. If this was "real-world politics," they wanted no part of it. Nor did they want any further part of Rustin, who they now viewed as a sellout. He had helped them mount a challenge to the established political order, only to jump to the side of the establishment, accepting the crumbs it offered instead of waging a principled battle for democracy and equality. Rustin was nothing more than Johnson's lackey.

The "compromise" that MFDP refused was implemented nonetheless. In a touch of irony that could not have been lost on Rustin, the regular Mississippi delegates, sensing the end of white supremacy in the Democratic Party, themselves walked out of the convention. At the next Democratic Convention in 1968, all delegates were selected on a nondiscriminatory basis, and in future years black Southerners would form a major Democratic constituency, without whom the party could not compete effectively in national elections. Indeed, by the 1970s, the Southern political landscape was almost unrecognizable from what it had been in 1964. It contained hundreds of black elected officials, a legacy of the Johnson-imposed compromise in Atlantic City. Rustin could envision this improved future, but MFDP's disillusioned leaders could not. His relationship with SNCC, which sponsored MFDP, did not recover. Rustin now believed that the road to his dream of racial equality and economic justice led through the Democratic Party, the same party SNCC viewed as racist, reactionary, and hypocritical. He maintained that SNCC's road—as well as that of CORE, which by 1964 was also moving toward separatism—led to a political and moral dead end and to the isolation and impotence of the self-righteous outsider. Their paths had permanently diverged.

Rustin's actions during the 1964 presidential general election campaign further estranged him from his former civil rights allies. Rustin was determined that President Johnson be reelected. His dreams were now tied to the mainstream wing of the Democratic Party, and the thought of a Republican victory in November chilled him. Republican nominee Barry Goldwater opposed both federal civil rights legislation and the use of federal power generally. The America Goldwater envisioned would be one in which states and localities made the essential decisions affecting their citizens' lives, allowing the inequities of the Jim Crow South to survive.

Under these circumstances, Rustin feared that civil rights activity, with its potential for unrest, could only hurt Johnson and aid Goldwater. In 1941, when the American Communist Party had ordered a halt to civil rights demonstrations to avoid impeding the war effort, Rustin had refused to comply and left the CPUSA over the issue. But now he made a different choice. He sponsored a moratorium on civil rights activity until Election Day in November, which he induced King, Randolph, Wilkins, and Whitney Young to endorse. Rustin emphasized that the moratorium would not extend to campaigning on behalf of the national Democratic ticket. SNCC and CORE, however, had soured on electoral politics in the wake of MFDP's failure to seat its delegates at the Democratic Convention. Their members refused to be bound by the moratorium agreement. To them, it was but another manifestation of a racist white power structure that bought the allegiance of former radicals like Rustin with empty promises of influence and access.

To Rustin's immense relief, Johnson won the November election in a rout. He carried forty-four states, losing only in Goldwater's home base of Arizona and the Deep South—Mississippi, Alabama, Louisiana, Georgia, and South Carolina. Although not quite the magnitude of Roosevelt's overwhelming 1936 victory, it was nonetheless an emphatic mandate for the president. Rustin was gratified by the apparent success of the civil rights moratorium. He was also greatly encouraged by the political realignment at work among the Democrats. The segregationists were clearly leaving, on their way to a new home in the Republican Party. He now saw a great opportunity for the Democratic Party to overcome its racist past and sponsor major civil rights and antipoverty initiatives. The same political, social, and economic transformations he had pursued from outside the established order for decades could now be realized from within. The Johnson victory and the hope it produced bound Rustin closer than ever to the president's wing of the Democratic Party.

But there was little joy within the ranks of SNCC and CORE, where the choice between Johnson and Goldwater, or between any Democrat and any Republican, was increasingly viewed as irrelevant. For both organizations, the Democratic Convention had marked the beginning of a journey away from integration, nonviolence—and Bayard Rustin. His new interest in traditional politics and apparent loss of faith in civil rights protest had driven a wedge between them. The coalition that had appeared so promising at the March on Washington only a year earlier was already beginning to splinter.

In February 1965, immediately after Johnson's inauguration, Rustin articulated his changing philosophy in an article published in *Commentary*, a left-of-center magazine, titled "From Protest to Politics: The Future of the Civil Rights Movement." Now that the legal supports of the Jim Crow system had been demolished through the efforts of civil rights demonstrators and the power of federal legislation, he argued that "what began as a protest movement is being challenged to translate itself into a political movement."[4] African Americans were poised to move within the traditional structures of American political life and to use established political channels to achieve their goals. Rustin believed that a unique moment in the nation's history was imminent. A revolutionary transformation of the American economic system through peaceful and democratic means was now possible. This was so because a constituency for change composed of white liberals, labor unions, religious groups, and African Americans now existed in the United States. The Johnson landslide, in Rustin's view, was proof of it. There was support for a huge federal attack on poverty and inequality in the United States, involving direct government management of the economy, an unprecedented level of social welfare expenditures, and an expansion of national power that would dwarf the New Deal.

Rustin warned that this transformation would not come to pass through demonstrations, but by the less dramatic work of negotiation, coalition, and compromise within the existing political system. With white Southerners deserting it in droves, the Democratic Party now belonged to the progressive forces that had coalesced at the March on Washington. The party could thus be the vehicle of the revolution Rustin had dreamed of for decades. By definition, party politics was slow, inefficient, and often frustrating. It was not the best of venues for those with deeply held principles. It rewarded the cynical, the insincere, and the corrupt. It demanded alliances of convenience with Democratic machine bosses such as Mayor Richard Daley of Chicago, as well as with the nation's ultimate practitioner of political hardball, Lyndon Johnson. As unpleasant as they often were, argued Rustin, these relationships nonetheless had to be built, because moral force by itself was not enough. "[T]he difference between expediency and morality in politics," he explained, "is the difference between

Rustin speaking in Harlem, 1965. Source: Library of Congress.

selling out a principle and making smaller concessions to win larger ones. . . . [T]here is a limit to what Negroes can do alone."[5]

The struggle for black voting rights in Selma, Alabama, which was reaching a climax as "From Protest to Politics" appeared in print, seemed to illustrate Rustin's point. King and the SCLC had made the town the center of their campaign to register black voters in the South in the early months of 1965. Selma thus became the site of the climactic battle for political control of the region. An enfranchised black population would destroy the white supremacist power structure in the South, and Alabama Governor George Wallace knew it. He fought desperately to prevent African Americans from becoming voters. Taking his cue from Wallace, Selma Sheriff Jim Clark had his men beat and jail blacks who appeared at the county courthouse and attempted to register. On March 7, 1965, what became known as "Bloody Sunday," Wallace's state troopers met demonstrators who were marching from Selma to the state capital of Montgomery with clubs and tear gas. The nationally televised violence galvanized support for federal voting rights legislation, which Johnson soon introduced. Rustin had been lobbying White House officials for such a law since the 1964 presidential election. He worked with the Johnson administration and with sympathetic congressional leaders over the next five months to beat back a Southern-led filibuster aimed at derailing it.

Rustin also served as an adviser to and spokesman for the Selma campaign, conferring regularly with King, obtaining financial contributions, and organizing rallies in Northern cities. On March 25, 1965, after completing the interrupted "Bloody Sunday" march from Selma to Montgomery with hundreds of supporters, King spoke on the steps of the Alabama State Capitol, with Rustin at his side. "The arc of the moral universe is long," he said, employing the words of another racial egalitarian, the nineteenth-century antislavery crusader Theodore Parker, "but it bends toward justice."[6] In August of that year, as if to bear him out, Congress passed the Voting Rights Act, which made the federal government the guarantor of black enfranchisement in the South and fulfilled the Fifteenth Amendment's 1870 promise of equality in the administration of the ballot. Thanks to this law and the Civil Rights Act of 1964, African Americans were poised not only to become first-class citizens of the United States at last, but also a critically important constituency in the Democratic Party, both as voters and officeholders. Rustin's dream of a politically empowered black population was about to be realized. No Democrat running for office would ever ignore them again.

Rustin stood behind President Johnson at the White House on August 6, 1965, and saw him place his signature on the Voting Rights Act, a symbol both of the triumph of the political revolution he had helped initiate and of the distance he had traveled personally. The road to the president's side had indeed been a long and unlikely one. It had wound through federal prison, a "morals" conviction, and dozens of poorly attended demonstrations for marginal causes. But the March on Washington had changed everything for Rustin. It had brought him into the American mainstream after years as an outsider. It had made it possible for the president of the United States to consider him an important ally during the push to get the Civil Rights and Voting Rights Acts through Congress. Rustin was now part of Johnson's "team," close enough to be invited to meetings at the White House and relied upon for electoral support.

Rustin's work for voting rights gave the philosophy he had expressed in "From Protest to Politics" practical application. It also completed his passage from the margins to the centers of power in U.S. politics and society. It accorded him influence within the mainstream liberal wing of the Democratic Party and access to the highest circles of government power. But many of Rustin's former colleagues viewed "From Protest to Politics" and his more accommodationist political stances as betrayals. They would not forgive what they considered his abandonment of principle for a seat at the table of a morally corrupt president. By 1965 opposition to the Vietnam War had galvanized and united leftists of all stripes, including pacifists, socialists, Communists, mainstream civil rights leaders, black nationalists, and perhaps most importantly, members of what was known as the New Left. A loosely defined amalgamation of students and young radicals harshly critical of capitalist exploitation and racial injustice at home and militarism and imperialism abroad, the New Left drew its numerical strength and ideological power from the Vietnam issue. SDS, its most prominent organization, was committed to an all-inclusive leftist politics, even welcoming old-line Communist Party supporters whom Rustin had shunned for decades.

Rustin was also deeply troubled by the war in Vietnam. By its very nature, it offended his pacifist sensibilities. It endangered the lives of hundreds of thousands of people of color in a developing nation. It diverted billions of dollars from the poor and working-class Americans to whom he had devoted his career as an activist. It epitomized the worst excesses of Cold War anti-Communist hysteria. But Vietnam was Johnson's war, and Rustin had placed his faith in the president. If there was to be true economic justice in the United States—if every American was to have a living income, a productive job, adequate health care—it would have to come from Johnson and his wing of the Democratic Party. Johnson did not hesitate to make support for his Vietnam position a test of loyalty, as King, with whom LBJ broke after he publicly opposed the war, learned painfully. Rustin felt he could not afford to take this chance. He was also concerned about the influence of Communists within SDS and the antiwar movement. This was perhaps an overreaction, given their relatively small numbers, but understandable from one with Rustin's disillusioning experiences with the Communist Party during the 1940s.

He thus muted his criticisms of the war, largely absenting himself from antiwar demonstrations and avoiding direct condemnations in public statements and in print. Pragmatism, it seemed to those in the pacifist and antiwar movements, had won out over principle. In the eyes of many who had worked with him previously, Rustin had made a cynical bargain with LBJ on the issue of the war. Former peace movement colleagues and New Leftists lashed out at him in the pages of *Liberation*, the journal Rustin had helped found. They accused him of breaking with the pacifist ideals that had shaped his life in order to curry favor with the Johnson administration.

But Rustin saw things differently. In keeping with the philosophy he had articulated in "From Protest to Politics," holding his tongue on Vietnam, as difficult as it was, represented a compromise in the interest of a larger goal. So it came to be that a man who until early 1965 was executive secretary of the War Resisters League chose the cause of economic justice over peace. Twenty years earlier he had gone to prison rather than support World War II, a crusade for human freedom and dignity. Now he was willing to overlook the consequences of a Vietnam War that most on the left viewed as manifestly immoral. If silence on the war issue was the price of staying in the good graces of the Johnson administration and keeping his dream of economic equality alive, Rustin was willing to pay it.

Rustin's turn toward establishment politics began to bring him tangible rewards in 1965. Having left the War Resisters League that year, he lacked a permanent organizational base and a steady source of income. Randolph stepped in, as he so often did when his friend needed him. By 1965 Randolph was the nation's preeminent black labor leader, and one of the few of any race to build a union from the ground up, as he had with the Brotherhood of Sleeping Car Porters. His ties to the AFL-CIO, the largest and most powerful labor union in the United States, were deep, and he decided to use them to help Rustin. The AFL-CIO agreed to honor Randolph by creating the A. Philip Randolph Institute, which it would help fund. The institute's main goal would be to maintain ties between the civil rights and labor movements, building on the momentum of the March on Washington. Randolph gave Rustin a permanent salaried position as the institute's executive secretary. He was now professionally and financially secure.

But just as his relationship with the Johnson administration made it difficult for him to speak freely about the war in Vietnam, the safe haven offered by the institute also curtailed his independence. As Rustin moved into the orbit of the mainstream labor movement, as exemplified by the AFL-CIO and George Meany, its cautious president, the sincerity of his political judgments were called into question. Rustin had spent the years preceding his emergence as a national figure in the 1960s taking principled stands on the issues he faced. Although some criticized his judgments, few challenged the depth of his convictions. But the support the Randolph Institute received from the AFL-CIO made Rustin's positions suspect in the eyes of many of his contemporaries in the civil rights and peace movements who were moving in more militant and confrontational directions by the mid-1960s. George Meany was a strong supporter of Johnson's position on the war in Vietnam and an opponent of black nationalism. Did Rustin's ties to the AFL-CIO affect his political judgments? Had he "sold out" to Meany and Johnson? These questions circulated among Rustin's former allies on the left for the rest of the decade and for the rest of his life.

One of the first initiatives proposed by Rustin through the A. Philip Randolph Institute was a massive expansion of the War on Poverty, which he called the "Freedom Budget." He had originally mentioned his idea for the Freedom Budget in November 1965 at a planning meeting for a White House conference on race that was scheduled for the following spring. Although the meeting and the conference itself reflected the growing divisions within the civil rights movement—SNCC and CORE representatives appeared only for the purpose of denouncing the president—Rustin was encouraged by the willingness of White House officials to at least consider large-scale government expenditures on social welfare programs and a greatly expanded War on Poverty.

Rustin officially announced the Freedom Budget in October 1966. It called for the federal government to spend $100 billion during the succeeding ten years on the most generous array of social services the nation had ever offered. The Freedom Budget's stated goal was to end poverty permanently in the United States. It would do so by pouring money into education and training programs, providing free medical care, guaranteeing every able-bodied citizen a decent-paying job, and making outright income grants to the needy. At the end of ten years, every American man, woman, and child would enjoy a standard of living that exceeded the official poverty line in the United States.

Rustin knew the Johnson administration and congressional Democrats would view the Freedom Budget as almost prohibitively expensive. He also faced the challenge of convincing the average American that the plan was feasible. Accordingly, he sought to cast the Freedom Budget in the most moderate terms possible, as an affordable measure that would not require significant redistribution of resources from middle- and upper-class Americans to the poor. Rustin argued, in fact, that no citizen would feel a significant financial burden under the Freedom Budget. In the promotional material he circulated nationally, Rustin wrote that its goals could be realized without tax increases, inflation, or any significant changes in the nation's economic system. The Freedom Budget would rely instead on the growth generated by an expanding economy to fund its programs. America's gross national product had been increasing yearly since the beginning of World War II a quarter century earlier. Rustin's assumption that it would continue to do so permitted him to forecast the availability of a ten-year, $100 billion surplus.

Rustin testifying before Congress with A. Philip Randolph, 1960s. Source: Corbis.

If Rustin had confined his arguments in favor of the Freedom Budget to economics, he might have attracted support for it on the left. But in his eagerness to prove that his plan was realistic, he maintained that it would not require a reduction in existing national defense expenditures. The United States could fund the Freedom Budget even if it continued to spend the sums necessary to continue the Vietnam War. Rustin did not intend this argument to be an endorsement of the war. He merely wished to show that the national economy was growing at a rate that would sustain the Freedom Budget along with all other current and future obligations.

In retrospect, however, this was a mistake. By 1966 and 1967, the war in Vietnam obsessed the American left. The conflict dominated its discourse, eclipsing even civil rights. SNCC and CORE were by this time all-black organizations, having expelled whites in the wake of their rejection of integrationism and nonviolence. Even the most committed white leftists were no longer welcome within the ranks of what was known by mid-decade as the black power movement. Black power, as articulated by leaders such as Stokely Carmichael, who replaced John Lewis as SNCC president in 1966, and Floyd McKissick, who took over for James Farmer as CORE's director the same year, emphasized cultural pride and the political and economic autonomy of the African American community. It equated nonviolence with weakness and accommodationism. By definition, black power excluded whites, and leftist refugees from SNCC, CORE, and other civil rights groups shifted their attention to the antiwar issue. Attacking the war in Vietnam offered white radicals, who militant blacks now viewed as part of a racist power structure, a degree of welcome moral certitude. They could criticize American militarism, imperialism, and racism as righteous outsiders free from personal responsibility for the crimes of the government.

Vietnam thus served both a political and a psychological purpose for white leftists. It also meant that they could not support any domestic policy initiative that could possibly be associated with the Johnson administration, even one as idealistic as the Freedom Budget. Rustin would be a casualty of their antipathy to the war. By arguing in effect that the United States could "afford" both the Freedom Budget and the war in Vietnam, Rustin appeared insufficiently antagonistic to an unjust conflict. Leftist politics in America had become increasingly simplistic. One was either unconditionally opposed to the war or considered an apologist for it. The Freedom Budget was thus doomed on the left virtually from the moment Rustin announced it. Rustin hated war, but he was unwilling to wait until peace was at hand to launch a crusade against poverty in the United States. Over the course of his career, he had repeatedly been forced to make choices between competing causes—peace, economic justice, civil rights. Now he was arguing that such a choice was unnecessary, and that the nation could spend amply both on the military and human needs. But this only enraged the antiwar left, which viewed the Freedom Budget as a form of blood money. Even the injustice of poverty paled in comparison with that of the war in Vietnam. Antiwar activists believed that Rustin had sold his soul on the war issue. All of LBJ's billions could not erase that stain.

By 1967 Rustin was estranged from almost all of the peace activists with whom he had worked in the Fellowship of Reconciliation and the War Resisters League. SDS and other New Left organizations regarded him as a turncoat and a Johnson puppet. Black nationalists, including members of SNCC and CORE, scorned him as a dupe of the white establishment. By this time as well, the economic pressures of the Vietnam War had made it impossible for the Johnson administration and Congress to even consider funding the Freedom Budget, and the rise of black power and the explosion of civil disturbances in the nation's black communities had destroyed the political will of white Americans to pay for expensive antipoverty measures.

The Watts riot of August 1965, which erupted in Los Angeles only days after Rustin had watched Johnson sign the Voting Rights Act, had deeply shaken whites, including many who had cheered King at the March on Washington. Leaving thirty-four dead and causing $35 million in property damage, Watts was the first in a series of violent outbreaks that would sweep through America's cities for the rest of the decade. The riots sparked a conservative counterreaction—labeled "white backlash"—that fueled substantial Republican Party gains in the congressional elections of 1966. Republican leaders dismissed the Freedom Budget as an example of wasteful liberal social spending. Rustin thus had almost no support for his vision of economic equality in America. The coalition upon which he had placed his hopes was in shambles.

Even King was keeping his distance. King also desired to end poverty in the United States, of course, but was much more willing than Rustin to articulate his demands from a position outside establishment political circles. By 1966 it was clear the two men were traveling in different directions. That year Rustin opposed King's first venture into the North, a planned Chicago campaign for jobs and open housing, arguing that confronting the powerful Democratic political machine of Mayor Richard Daley was a mistake. In 1967 Rustin counseled King against taking a public stand against the war in Vietnam, advice the minister ignored. Rustin even criticized the more confrontational strategies of King's 1968 Poor People's Campaign, which shared the Freedom Budget's antipoverty goals, but relied on the nonviolent direct action tactics that Rustin now questioned. The campaign's planned sit-ins, he advised, would only alienate the Democratic legislators in whose hands the solution to America's poverty problem lay. King never stopped listening to Rustin, but after 1965 he took his advice less and less. He believed that Rustin was a well-meaning man who had been seduced by establishment power and lost his way.

By the late 1960s, only a few years removed from the March on Washington and its grand possibilities, Rustin's dream seemed as remote as it had been during his decades on the margins. The principles that had seemed settled at the march—interracialism, economic equality, nonviolence—were now in the air. Rustin faced a radicalized left, a separatist black power movement, a conservative-trending white middle and working class, and a Democratic Party unwilling to spend the sums necessary to fight a meaningful War on Poverty. He had resolved to work within the existing political structure, building coalitions, making pragmatic decisions, compromising principles, seeking power. Rustin was now welcome in the offices of mayors, governors, congressmen, and the president of the United States. But what had he accomplished?

The United States was more violent and divided, less generous and optimistic. Gross disparities remained in the nation's economic and social structure. America seemed to be dissolving into a series of disconnected agendas, united only by anger. Rustin, almost alone among his contemporaries, was able to craft a broad vision that integrated political, economic, and social change. Yet in most quarters of the left, he was no longer even thought of as a "radical." With the Freedom Budget campaign at a standstill and his influence on the left and within the civil rights movement waning, Rustin turned to the one element of the March on Washington coalition that still welcomed him—organized labor—and invested his American dream in it.

It is tempting to attribute Rustin's intense loyalty to the labor movement to the financial assistance it offered the Randolph Institute and its initiatives, especially the Freedom Budget. But there was more to it than this. In the early years of the twentieth century, the English working class mobilized politically through the vehicle of the British Labour Party. By 1950 union leaders had become elected Labour Party officials and helped pass programs that guaranteed British citizens an array of cradle-to-grave services protecting them from want, hunger, idleness, and illness. Rustin designed the Freedom Budget as an American version of what the British Labour Party had accomplished. He understood that, as in Great Britain, any hope for economic justice in the United States rested with the labor movement.

Rustin knew that the history of organized labor in America was tinged with racism. African Americans were routinely barred from locals affiliated with the American Federation of Labor (AFL), the nation's preeminent labor organization during the late nineteenth and twentieth centuries. Forced into roles as strikebreakers, blacks were targeted by white employees fearing for their jobs.

But more recent developments gave Rustin cause for optimism. The Congress of Industrial Organizations (CIO), founded in 1935 to unionize unskilled and semiskilled workers in the nation's heavy manufacturing sector, featured a strong commitment to civil rights. It merged with the AFL in 1955, and although instances of racial exclusion persisted in the AFL-CIO into the 1970s, they were clearly on the decline. Many of the member unions of the AFL-CIO, in fact, had rallied in support of Rustin's economic and civil rights agenda at the March on Washington. The AFL-CIO also strongly supported the Civil Rights Act of 1964 and Voting Rights Act of 1965. AFL-CIO unions such as the UAW, the UFT, and A. Philip Randolph's Brotherhood of Sleeping Car Porters, among others, were substantial financial contributors to King and the SCLC. Many labor leaders, including the UAW's Walter Reuther, Albert Shanker of the UFT, and the Sleeping Car Porters' Randolph, had ties to the socialist movement and were sympathetic to its goals.

These leaders were also committed to achieving economic and racial justice through collective bargaining and the electoral process and building the same coalitions with African Americans, religious groups, and liberal Democratic politicians whom Rustin favored. Only within the ranks of organized labor did there appear to be an understanding that America could not be true to its egalitarian principles as long as sharp class divisions existed among its citizens. Union leaders believed, as Rustin did, that the way to make Americans "equal" was not through racial or ethnic identity politics, but by equalizing incomes. They, like Rustin, had grown impatient with an antiwar movement whose narrow focus crowded out serious consideration of class issues. Vietnam, AFL-CIO officials believed, had become a distraction for the left, a way to avoid the problem of economic inequality. Ending the war in Vietnam would not end poverty in the United States—enacting the Freedom Budget would.

Rustin also felt an affinity with most labor leaders on civil rights issues. By the late 1960s he had become a vocal critic of black power ideology. Its avowal of separatism ran counter to Rustin's integrationism, of course; but just as damaging in his view was its intellectual shallowness. Black power substituted style and slogan for substance and strategy. Rustin ridiculed the notion that feelings of racial pride and identity could improve the lives of African Americans in the absence of billions in antipoverty spending. The aggrieved self-righteousness of black power advocates such as SNCC's Stokely Carmichael and CORE's Floyd McKissick, who by 1966 had endorsed racial separatism, deeply offended him. Black power, Rustin charged in a *Commentary* article published that year, was a posture and not a program.[7] It would only drive away liberal whites whose support blacks desperately needed, leaving them at the mercy of Southern racists and Republican Party reactionaries. He and his labor allies agreed that it was economic and not cultural radicalism that could save black America.

The labor movement thus offered Rustin a congenial home when other doors were closed to him. It fit his outlook and sensibilities perfectly. That the AFL-CIO's Meany was bankrolling the Randolph Institute was not the most important explanation for Rustin's embrace of mainstream labor during the later half of the 1960s, whatever his disillusioned former colleagues on the left may have believed. Ideologically, it represented his last remaining sanctuary. Increasingly cut off from the antiwar and civil rights movements, he had nowhere else to go.

By 1968 Rustin was operating the Randolph Institute out of the headquarters of the UFT on Park Avenue South in New York City. The union, which represented the city's 55,000 public schoolteachers, was a generous contributor to the institute. Rustin's friendship with UFT president Albert Shanker made the tenancy arrangement a logical one. But there was a more compelling reason for their physical proximity. The UFT was embroiled in a racially incendiary battle over "community control" of schools in New York City's black neighborhoods, and Rustin was virtually the only prominent African American to support the union.

Conditions in the New York public schools had long concerned Rustin. In 1964 his pro-integration boycott had failed to yield substantive results. Four years later, the city schools were still racially segregated. They were also still shortchanging black pupils, who were taught by inexperienced or incompetent teachers in decrepit, dangerous, and overcrowded buildings. But a new movement with roots in the African American neighborhoods of the city had emerged to offer hope for change. After Rustin's 1964 boycott, frustrated black parents began to argue that if their local schools could not be integrated, they, and not the central board of education, should control them. Their demand for "community control" of education in African American areas quickly became a rallying cry for marginalized black New Yorkers across the city. On its surface, the community control idea seemed appealing. It would empower African Americans and give them a sense of pride and identity. It would help unite their transient, fractured neighborhoods and might even lead to educational innovation. The city's white public schoolteachers did not seem to understand how to reach black students. Perhaps it was time to give African Americans themselves a chance.

In the spring of 1967, responding to pressure from black parents and activists, the city's board of education announced that it would conduct experiments in community control of education in three minority neighborhoods. One of them was Ocean Hill-Brownsville, a predominantly black area in Brooklyn with some of the worst-performing schools in the city. That summer Ocean Hill-Brownsville residents elected a governing board to run their schools. It claimed sweeping powers, including the right to hire and fire teachers. The UFT, fearing for the job security of its members, objected. The union and the governing board sparred over the issue during the 1967–1968 school year, in an increasingly ugly racial atmosphere.

The UFT was a strong supporter of civil rights causes and an ally of King, but it was overwhelmingly white. Only 8 percent of the teachers in the New York public school system were black, among the lowest percentages of any American city.[8] The UFT was also newly established and insecure. Four years earlier, its leaders had refused to join Rustin's school boycott because they believed it threatened the survival of the union. Now, UFT President Albert Shanker viewed community control in similar terms. Since his teachers were protected by tenure and contractual due-process guarantees, handing over personnel powers to the Ocean Hill-Brownsville governing board would imperil the union's existence. Matters came to a head on May 9, 1968, when the Ocean Hill-Brownsville governing board, seeking to test its power, terminated nineteen white UFT teachers. After a fruitless summer of negotiations aimed at restoring the teachers to their positions, Shanker called a citywide UFT strike on September 9. There would be three strikes in all, affecting almost one million schoolchildren and causing substantial damage to the city's economy. The final UFT strike did not end until mid-November.

The Ocean Hill-Brownsville strikes were the most racially divisive events in the modern history of New York City. This alone would have presented Rustin with wrenching choices. But the class issues that were also embedded in the dispute pushed Rustin to the crossroads of his life as an activist. The Ocean Hill-Brownsville strikes forced civil rights and labor rights into conflict in ways Rustin could not avoid, setting the demands of race and class against each other. Rustin had fought for years to improve education for black youth in New York. He knew that they were cheated in comparison to white students, and had seen with his own eyes the stunted lives that resulted from second-rate schools and teachers. He viewed public education as an important civil rights issue. Opposing community control meant turning his back on the city's African American population, which overwhelmingly supported the actions of the Ocean Hill-Brownsville governing board.

But Rustin was also passionately loyal to labor and the UFT. His commitment to worker rights was as deep and long standing as that to civil rights. The Ocean Hill-Brownsville teachers had been fired without formal charges or hearings. A union that could not defend its members under these circumstances was not worthy of its name. Unions were the foundation upon which Rustin's dream of economic justice in the United States rested. Opposing the UFT meant turning his back on the American worker.

Rustin was also suspicious of community control as a principle. It explicitly abandoned his lifelong goal of racial integration. It was exclusionary and narrow, the very opposite of the open society he envisioned. With its emphasis on local autonomy, it reminded him of the "states' rights" philosophy employed by Southern segregationists against federal civil rights initiatives. Rustin believed, in fact, that community control perfectly suited the purposes of whites resisting school integration in New York, since they could also demand it for their segregated neighborhoods.

Rustin with UFT President Albert Shanker during the Ocean Hill-Brownsville dispute, 1968. Source: Corbis.

As the first UFT strike began in September, Rustin was faced with an awful choice. The union or the black community? Labor rights or civil rights? Supporting the UFT meant excusing racism, especially in view of the fact that New York's white middle class, much of which steadfastly opposed integrating the city's schools, had lined up solidly behind the union. But supporting the Ocean Hill-Brownsville governing board meant acting as a strikebreaker—as a "scab," the epithet reserved for betrayers of labor movements. Every major union in the city stood with Shanker and his teachers. Moreover, Manhattan-based business, professional, media, and intellectual leaders, as well as Mayor John Lindsay, a wealthy, Yale-educated reformer, championed community control and the governing board. They attacked the teachers for conducting what they viewed as a racially motivated strike against the African American community. Rustin, however, was contemptuous of these leaders. He considered them upper-class enemies of working people, representatives of "the bosses" who invariably sought to destroy unions.

Thus the competing claims of class and race, which Rustin had attempted to keep separate throughout his career as an activist, converged with brutal finality at Ocean Hill-Brownsville. The UFT strikes symbolized the end of his dream of a unified American radicalism. Blacks, whites, workers, the poor—Rustin believed they could all be brought together, that their similarities outweighed their differences. Ocean Hill-Brownsville proved him wrong. Rustin now had to choose among them. In so doing, he would leave a part of his dream behind forever. Whatever he decided, there could be no return to the way things had been. Either his career in civil rights or in the labor movement was over.

Rustin chose to support the UFT. He struggled desperately to keep racial considerations out of his position on the dispute. Soon after the strikes began in September, he drafted a statement that he placed in the city's major newspapers and induced a number of black labor officials to endorse it. In it, he argued that the sole principle at stake was that of "due process" for illegally terminated workers.[9] The strikes were about class issues and not race. If the fired teachers had been black instead of white, Rustin maintained, the union would also have struck to protect their rights. But Rustin was not being realistic. Striking white teachers and black counter demonstrators were confronting each other on a daily basis in front of schools across the city. Vile racial rhetoric flew in both directions. Police were often needed to keep the two sides from coming to blows. White UFT partisans called a black governing board supporter a "nigger scab," and another a "cannibal."[10] A flyer produced in the black community labeled the terminated UFT teachers, most of whom were Jewish, "Middle East Murderers of Colored People."[11] The mutual economic interests and shared humanity of poor and working-class New Yorkers seemed no longer to matter. Racial allegiances now overwhelmed all else. It was Rustin's worst nightmare come to life.

The black unionists Rustin had gathered in support of the UFT began to peel away almost immediately. By the middle of October most of those who had lent their names to his pro-union statement of the previous month had instead embraced community control and the Ocean Hill-Brownsville governing board. The city's African American labor leaders now refused to "support the teachers against (our) black brothers in the ghetto."[12] They turned against Rustin, attacking a man who helped integrate the United States military, counseled Martin Luther King, Jr., at Montgomery, planned the March on Washington, and was instrumental in the passage of the Civil Rights and Voting Rights Acts as a traitor to his race. Rustin, charged a black union official, had "sold out. Whatever you have done in the past, you have destroyed."[13] Another said he identified first as an African American and only secondarily as a labor man. The unionists agreed that Rustin now spoke only for himself and not for any significant segment of the black population.

The reaction to Rustin's support of the UFT was equally intense and negative within the city's African American population as a whole. He received a barrage of angry letters from governing board supporters, accusing him of doing the work of the white power structure. One reminded him "that you were black even before you were male or American."[14] His race treason, she added, "deeply wounds many of us who for years admired and respected you for the leadership you have given to many unpopular causes."[15] A second critic complained "where blacks are concerned, you inevitably align yourself with the 'Establishment.' When one does this, can he really be called a 'Negro Leader'?"[16] Even moderate black officials like Whitney Young of the Urban League labeled Shanker a racist and took public stands against the UFT. Although Randolph remained loyal to him, Rustin was now isolated from the civil rights movement and his own people.

But Rustin held to his choice. He published pro-UFT articles and letters, appeared on television and radio, and stood by Shanker's side at press conferences and rallies. Often he was the only black face on the platform. Rustin continued to maintain that the dispute was a battle for labor rights and not civil rights. When the strikes ended with the forced return of the terminated teachers to the Ocean Hill-Brownsville schools on November 19 and the victory of the UFT, he shared labor's triumph with Shanker. Soon afterward, the Ocean Hill-Brownsville governing board was replaced and the community control experiment discontinued. The cost, however, had been horrific. By the end of the strikes, Shanker was being compared to Adolf Hitler in New York's black community. And Rustin had virtually no standing left in that community. The Randolph Institute would continue to offer him an income and a platform for his beliefs, but he never again wielded significant influence among black Americans.

In April 1968, King, with whom Rustin had maintained a respectful personal relationship even as their policy differences grew, was assassinated during an appearance on behalf of striking black sanitation workers in Memphis, Tennessee. He would be unavailable in the future to help Rustin navigate the hostile waters of African American public opinion. After King's death, Rustin worked briefly for the Poor People's Campaign that King had planned but did not live to see. In May and June, protesters occupied the Mall in Washington, only steps away from the site of the "I Have a Dream" speech. But there was no repeat of the grand accomplishments of August 28, 1963. Rustin clashed with the campaign's new leader, Ralph Abernathy, and resigned after he ignored Rustin's advice to articulate a set of concrete goals and enforce discipline among the increasingly unruly participants. The campaign ended in failure soon after Rustin left.

During the 1968 presidential election, Rustin attempted to drum up support in the black community for Hubert Humphrey, the Democratic candidate and Johnson's vice president. He had worked with Humphrey at the 1964 Democratic Convention during the controversy over seating the MFDP delegation, and the two were close political allies. As he had in 1964, Rustin feared the consequences of a Republican victory. Richard Nixon, the Republican Party candidate, was no friend of civil rights, nor was George Wallace, the segregationist former Alabama governor who was running as an independent. This time, Rustin's fears were realized. He was unable to bring out enough African American voters for Humphrey to prevent Nixon from winning the presidency in November, around the time the Ocean Hill-Brownsville strikes were ending.

With Nixon's inauguration in January 1969, the modern civil rights era in the United States came to an end. Rustin was as responsible for the successes of that era as any American. Jim Crow was dead, black voting rights guaranteed, and a War on Poverty launched. Martin Luther King, Jr., an African American, was regarded as the nation's preeminent moral leader by Americans of all races. President John Kennedy had appeared on national television and described racial discrimination as an issue "as old as the Scriptures and . . . as clear as the American Constitution."[17] His successor, Lyndon Johnson, had stood before Congress and repeated the civil rights movement's own motto: "We shall overcome."[18]

Rustin had played a major role in all these milestones. Yet as the 1960s concluded, he was without honor in his own community. His dream of an interracial movement for economic justice in the United States, one that had shone so brightly at the March on Washington, was dead. Rustin now faced the bitter truth that to the majority of Americans race, not class, counted most. He had hoped to use the civil rights movement to create a nation in which the color of one's skin did not matter, and simultaneously use the labor movement to build an America without class distinctions. But along the road to a color-blind, classless society, awful choices arose between equally worthy components of the same dream. Rustin's choice of labor rights over civil rights at Ocean Hill-Brownsville was courageous and farsighted, because he understood that class identities could bind Americans together in ways that those based on race could not. His decision was a profoundly human one. But humanists are not always rewarded in their own time. At decade's end, Rustin had paid dearly for his humanity and vision.

Notes

1. Leonard Buder, "Boycott Cripples City Schools," *New York Times*, February 4, 1964, pp. 1, 29; Leonard Buder, "Move to Mediate School Dispute in City Rebuffed," *New York Times*, February 5, 1964, p. 1.

2. Buder, "Boycott," *New York Times*, February 4, 1964, pp. 1, 29; Buder, "Move to Mediate," *New York Times*, February 5, 1964, p. 1.

3. William A. DeGregorio, *The Complete Book of U.S. Presidents*, 4th ed. (New York: Barricade Books, 1993), p. 490.

4. Bayard Rustin, "From Protest to Politics: The Future of the Civil Rights Movement," *Commentary*, 39 (February 1965): 26.

5. Rustin, "From Protest to Politics, pp. 29, 31.

6. Clayborne Carson and Kris Shepard, eds., *A Call to Conscience: The Landmark Speeches of Dr. Martin Luther King, Jr.* (New York: Warner Books, 2001), p. 131.

7. Bayard Rustin, "'Black Power' and Coalition Politics," *Commentary*, 42 (September 1966): 35–40.

8. Jerald Podair, *The Strike that Changed New York: Blacks, Whites, and the Ocean Hill-Brownsville Crisis* (New Haven, CT: Yale University Press, 2002), p. 155.

9. A. Philip Randolph Institute, "An Appeal to the Community from Black Trade Unionists," *New York Times*, September 19, 1968, p. 39.

10. Podair, *The Strike that Changed New York*, pp. 135, 137.

11. Podair, *The Strike that Changed New York*, p. 124.

12. Letter, William Cross to Harry Van Arsdale, November 2, 1968, New York Central Labor Council Papers, Box 19, Robert F. Wagner Labor Archives, New York University, New York, NY.

13. Podair, *The Strike that Changed New York*, p. 135.

14. Letter, Thelma Griffith to Bayard Rustin, September 20, 1968, Bayard Rustin Papers, Reel 6, Frame 62. Library of Congress, Washington, DC.

15. Letter, Thelma Griffith to Bayard Rustin.

16. Letter, John Hunter to Bayard Rustin, September 25, 1968, Bayard Rustin Papers, Reel 6, Frame 189. Library of Congress, Washington, DC.

17. Clayborne Carson, et al., eds., *Eyes on the Prize: America's Civil Rights Years* (New York: Penguin, 1987), p. 120.

18. *Public Papers of the Presidents of the United States, Lyndon Johnson, 1965* (Washington, DC: U.S. Government Printing Office, 1966), p. 284.

CHAPTER FIVE

~

The Humanist, 1969–1987

Bayard Rustin never stopped regarding himself as a revolutionary, whatever others may have thought. He continued to view his activities during the 1970s and 1980s in these terms. He was no longer considered a "spokesman" for African Americans or a "civil rights leader." But almost paradoxically, this may have liberated him. He could now broaden the scope of his dreams to help "people in trouble" whomever and wherever they were. In the final decades of his life, he was at last free to be a humanist—one who seeks justice for all, not just for "his own."

Rustin's work during this period took him all over the world. Domestic politics in the United States was shifting rightward, to his disappointment. Republican presidents occupied the White House for all but four years of the 1970s and 1980s. Richard Nixon, Gerald Ford, and, especially, Ronald Reagan, convinced much of the American electorate that the federal government was the cause of, and not the solution to, the nation's economic and social ills. Nixon ended most of the War on Poverty programs that Rustin hoped would be a first step on the road to his egalitarian agenda. With his emphasis on free markets and the private sector, Reagan changed the nation's political culture in a way that shattered Rustin's dream of guaranteed jobs and incomes for all Americans. Under these inauspicious circumstances, it would not have been surprising if Rustin lost faith in the popular will, in the ability of average citizens to govern themselves. Certainly many of his former allies on the left had done so. But his lifelong allegiance to democratic values did not waver in his final years.

In the 1970s Rustin developed an association with Freedom House, a group that promoted open elections and human rights internationally. A bipartisan organization begun during World War II to control the abuses of dictatorial regimes, it sponsored missions to supervise voting processes and protect civil liberties in struggling democracies. Freedom House was particularly critical of Marxist and Soviet-backed regimes, a stance that matched Rustin's. Years of attacks from New Leftists, Vietnam War opponents, and his erstwhile colleagues in the peace movement had hardened his already strong anti-Communist sensibilities. A man who had been a harsh critic of the Cold War in the 1940s and 1950s now had become a tough-minded Cold Warrior himself. Rustin's Freedom House work allowed him to oppose Marxism and build democracy at the same time.

The countries to which he traveled on his Freedom House missions were hardly fertile soil for the growth of democracy. Some, like Haiti, had been independent nations for many years, but were wracked by political violence and ruled by repressive dictatorships that employed secret police to intimidate dissidents. Others, like Zimbabwe, the former Rhodesia, had only recently emerged from British colonialism and had no democratic heritage. Still others, like Chile, were long-functioning democracies that had been subverted by military coups. And South Africa was an apartheid state, with democracy for whites only.

Rustin approached these and other nations he visited, including El Salvador, Lebanon, Paraguay, and Barbados, in the same pragmatic spirit that marked his post–March on Washington politics. He helped supervise elections that would not have been considered fair by American standards. In Zimbabwe in 1979, he agreed to certify a U.S. government-backed prime ministerial candidate whose campaign tactics were less than above board. Rustin reasoned that in a political system where all actors were to some degree ethically compromised, the fact that elections were held at all meant success. But when a Marxist won the Zimbabwean prime ministry the following year, Rustin was more critical of the process and more pessimistic about the chances for the development of free institutions in the future. His adversaries on the left attributed Rustin's negative reaction to this election to his Cold War politics. They believed that he was now so invested in anti-Soviet ideology that he could not accept a Marxist electoral victory on any terms.

This was partially true. Rustin's antipathy toward communism, almost four decades old, had by this last phase of his career reached a full boil. But his impulses were not so easily categorized. He believed in democracy's transformative power with a sincerity that many on the left, for all their invocations of the virtues of "the people," did not share. This faith was at the heart of Rustin's anticommunism. Marxism, in his view, made men and women less human. Under the guise of providing for their material needs, it destroyed the possibility of independent thought, choice, and growth. By subordinating the rights of the individual to the state, it created a climate weighted with fear and suspicion. Rustin felt that democracy helped human beings realize their potential, while Marxism left them stunted and unfulfilled. Moreover, Communist regimes differed from those run by authoritarian strongmen who sought simply to exercise power and not impose an ideology. Dictators could be overthrown and replaced by democracies, but Communist states endured over time, unchanging. Rustin needed only to look to the Soviet Union itself and its Eastern European satellite nations for any proof he needed in this regard.[1] Thus, in Zimbabwe and elsewhere, Rustin was more willing to accept the results of an election that installed an anti-Soviet leader than a Marxist one because he trusted even a flawed democracy to grow over time.

On his travels for Freedom House, Rustin learned to take situations as he found them. Chile, whose democratically elected Marxist government had been overthrown by a U.S.-backed military coup in 1973, was an obvious example of human rights violations, as was apartheid South Africa. A younger Rustin would have taken the leaders of both countries to task on moral grounds. Now, however, while continuing to work for justice, he resolved to do what he could with what he had before him. He refused to join the calls for complete divestment from apartheid South Africa that were circulating on the American left during the 1980s. Instead, he advocated building democratic institutions from the ground up through collaborations between labor unions, civil rights groups, and political parties in the United States and South Africa. Rustin believed that wholly apart from its moral failings, apartheid was unsustainable in a world where, thanks in large part to the U.S. civil rights movement, social equality was becoming the norm. Black majority rule would come to South Africa, of that he was convinced. But would the new South Africa be a clone of the dictatorships and failed Marxist states that dotted the continent's landscape? By engaging the nation Rustin was not accommodating the apartheid regime, as his critics charged, but seeding free institutions that could one day grow into a democratic South Africa.

Rustin applied the same flexible approach in Chile, where the military government of General Augusto Pinochet had banned free elections, muzzled the press, and committed gross human rights violations, including arbitrary arrests, torture, and murder. Rustin again chose to take small steps toward restoring democracy in Chile rather than joining most on the American left in issuing blanket condemnations of the regime. He worked quietly with Chilean labor leaders, journalists, and opposition leaders to moderate the actions of the Pinochet dictatorship and prepare the ground for the eventual return of democratic rule.

As before, Rustin's leftist critics interpreted his overtures to the Chilean government as a form of appeasement and reflexive anticommunism. They were correct to point out that Rustin's position was colored by his disapproval of the Marxist leader who had been deposed by the military coup and the fact that the resolutely anti-Communist Pinochet was a reliable U.S. Cold War ally. But Rustin was no more a Pinochet apologist than he was a defender of apartheid in South Africa. He sought to navigate the ground between the unquestioning support of all anti-Soviet states, which was the hallmark of the Nixon, Ford, and Reagan administrations, and the American left's uncritical posture toward Marxist regimes in the 1970s and 1980s. As an anti-Communist and a supporter of democracy, Rustin found that ground to be narrow indeed. But his belief in the ability of men and women wherever they lived to answer the questions of their own lives distinguished him from both the American foreign policy estab-lishment and the left. Freedom House allowed him to express this belief in de-mocracy on a global stage.

The last two decades of Rustin's life also offered the opportunity to help "people in trouble" through refugee assistance. His vehicle was the Interna-tional Rescue Committee (IRC), which had originally been formed to bring Jews out of Nazi-era Germany in the 1930s, and by the 1970s and 1980s had be-come an organization of worldwide scope. As he had in his work for Freedom House, Rustin combined anti-Communist and humanitarian impulses in his ef-forts on behalf of the IRC. He focused his attentions on Southeast Asia in the aftermath of the war in Vietnam, which ended with the victory of the Commu-nist North Vietnamese in 1975. That year, Cambodia was also conquered by Marxists in the form of the Khmer Rouge, a group of agrarian guerrilla fighters who launched a campaign of mass murder that eventually claimed between 1.5 and 2 million lives. South Vietnamese and Laotian Hmong, fearing reprisals for their support of the United States during the Vietnam conflict, along with Cambodians fleeing genocide in their own country, crowded into a series of refugee camps in neighboring Thailand.

Rustin posing with refugee children in a Thailand camp on an International Rescue Committee mission, 1979. Source: Estate of Bayard Rustin.

Rustin made numerous trips to the camps, which were administered by the United Nations and the IRC, in the late 1970s and 1980s. Although he attempted to improve living conditions there for the refugees—shelter, food, medical supplies—his role was not that of the typical bureaucrat. Circulating among the families, learning their names, hearing their stories, telling his own, Rustin was at peace with himself, beyond ideology, a humanist. Photographs from the trips show him relaxed and content, clearly doing work he enjoyed. He had spent his life trying to help other people, but often politics—the contradictions between the elements of his dream—interfered. In Thailand, nothing got in the way.

Rustin used the contacts he had established with U.S. government officials and union leaders to resettle the refugees in the United States. His efforts during the 1960s to remain in the good graces of the Democratic Party establishment and organized labor had cost him his standing on the American left, but they now bore fruit in support for his humanitarian work. Rustin had an impressive list of senators, congressmen, White House officials, and high-ranking union leaders who owed him favors, and he called in some of these debts on behalf of the refugees. In 1978 he made personal appeals to Vice President Walter Mondale and AFL-CIO President George Meany and pleaded the refugees' case to the House Judiciary Committee. He found a sympathetic audience. The AFL-CIO modified its traditional position against importing foreign labor, and the Jimmy Carter administration agreed to increase immigration quotas for the Asian refugees. Thanks to Rustin, thousands of displaced persons from Southeast Asia came to the United States and began new lives. Rustin's IRC refugee work probably gave him more personal satisfaction than anything else he had done in a long career as an activist.

Another instance of "people in trouble" involved Soviet Jews. Rustin's relationship with the American Jewish community had always been close. He had worked with Jews in the socialist and pacifist movements, and during the Ocean Hill-Brownsville school strikes of 1968 when Rustin supported the predominantly Jewish UFT against New York's black community. In many respects, the plight of Jews in the Soviet Union reminded Rustin of that of blacks in the United States. Victims of discrimination in employment, education, and housing, Jews were the objects of deep-seated and historic prejudices in Soviet society. They were also virtual prisoners in their own country, denied the opportunity to emigrate by the authorities.

During the 1970s Rustin became a vocal leader in the movement to bring Jews out of the Soviet Union and to resettle them in Israel. He worked with Senator Henry Jackson of Washington, who had introduced legislation tying trade relations with the Soviets to their treatment of Jews. The Jackson-Vanik Amendment to the 1974 Trade Act of the United States, introduced by the

Senator and Congressman Charles Vanik of Ohio, became law the next year. Aimed primarily at the Soviet Union, it restricted trade relations with nations that blocked the right to emigrate. Rustin was a tireless advocate for the amendment, speaking before congressional committees and in the media. He used the resources of the Randolph Institute to pay for advertisements and columns in newspapers and to cosponsor rallies. Eventually, the pressures of the Jackson-Vanik Amendment forced the Soviet Union to permit approximately one million of its Jews to leave for Israel.

Rustin's efforts on behalf of Soviet Jews meant more conflict with the New Left, to which the issue smacked of Cold War posturing. To Rustin, however, the oppression of Jews in the Soviet Union was a civil rights issue—a human rights issue. He would demonstrate the same level of moral passion for Afghan refugees fleeing the 1979 Soviet invasion of their country, Ethiopians displaced by a civil war, and El Salvadorans uprooted by misery and terror. These were not Rustin's "people," any more than were Hmong or Soviet Jews. They were, however, people, and that is what mattered to him. The mark of a true humanist is working on behalf of those in need simply because they are human. By the 1970s and 1980s, Rustin was estranged from the U.S. civil rights movement. But that movement had itself shrunk, replacing its universalist message with one based on the demands of African Americans as an interest group. It defined "justice" in these narrower, racialized terms. Rustin, however, had transcended this definition in his work for refugees and other "people in trouble." In his time of exile, he had become the most authentic civil rights leader of all.

Rustin's support for Soviet Jews was a major part of his effort to reanimate the alliance between blacks and Jews that had been so effective during the early days of the civil rights movement, and at the March on Washington. Their bonds had frayed after 1965 with the rise of black power ideology and had unraveled completely at Ocean Hill-Brownsville in 1968. His sympathy for the underdog motivated his support for Soviet Jewry, as well as for Israel, a fragile social democracy surrounded by hostile, Soviet-supported autocracies. But most black Americans viewed Jews, and Israel, in a harsher light. By the 1960s Jews had largely escaped the ghettos they often shared with blacks and planted themselves in the American white middle class as professionals, businessmen, and educators. They lived alongside other whites, segregated from African Americans by lines of race, culture, and geography. The only Jews with whom blacks came into contact on an everyday basis were representatives of the white power structure in their neighborhoods, including landlords, store owners, and, as the Ocean Hill-Brownsville dispute illustrated so painfully, teachers. It was thus difficult for Rustin to convince African Americans to think of Jews as partners in oppression.

Nor did blacks share Rustin's affinity for Israel. They saw the country as a proxy for America's imperialist designs in the Middle East and an instrument of racism against dark-skinned Arabs. As the issue of Palestinian autonomy gained steam in the 1970s, criticism of Israel mounted among blacks in the United States. Rustin was never able to induce more than a handful of black leaders to join him in his overtures to the American Jewish community. He was, ironically, more popular in that community during this period than he was among blacks. Some civil rights activists, in fact, regarded him as a captive of "Jewish interests" and a mouthpiece for the "Israel lobby." Rustin's ties to Jews and to Israel, then, only served to isolate him further from his own racial roots. Yet, by once again taking up the cause of "others," Rustin reaffirmed his humanism in a society in which racial, ethnic, and religious groups routinely confused "justice for all" with justice for them alone. His understanding of the interconnectedness of human beings overcame the confines of identity politics, and represented a vital, if unrealized, part of his dream. As he had so often during his career, Rustin paid a price for envisioning a world his contemporaries could not see.

Rustin's criticisms of affirmative action and university black studies programs during the last two decades of his life also reflected this vision. He continued to view economic injustice as the nation's most pressing issue. It affected Americans of all races and brought them together on common ground. The racial quotas of affirmative action, Rustin argued, did not address the fundamental question of wealth distribution in America. They shifted limited resources from the white working class to middle-class blacks, leaving the black poor largely as they were. The solution for Rustin lay not in offering a few crumbs to an arbitrarily selected group, but in sharing the nation's wealth with all of its citizens on an equal basis. In testimony before Congress in 1974, he argued "an affirmative action program cannot find jobs for the unemployed or help the underemployed into better jobs if those jobs do not exist. The most important issue is an economy of growth and expansion. Above all, it must be an economy providing jobs for all."[2] Affirmative action, for all its pretensions to making Americans "equal," would not end poverty in the United States. And as long as poverty persisted, all the racial quotas colleges and corporations could offer would not make America a truly egalitarian nation.

In addition, Rustin believed that quotas permitted upper-class whites to use their money and power to avoid making any substantial sacrifices on behalf of racial redress, placing the entire burden on those lower on the socioeconomic scale. Quotas thus destroyed any possibility for an interracial united front against economic injustice in the United States by pitting black and white workers against each other. "What the imposition of quotas, and the resulting furor they have generated, have accomplished," Rustin asserted in his 1974 congressional testimony, "is to exacerbate the differences between blacks and other racial and ethnic groups."[3] The national debate over affirmative action once again forced considerations of racial loyalty and class solidarity against each other, and Rustin's opposition to quotas set him further apart from prevailing sentiment in the American black community. Even elements within the NAACP, including the group's labor director Herbert Hill, criticized him for appearing to support white privilege in the nation's employment market.[4] But even at the cost of making more enemies, Rustin maintained his position on racial quotas for the rest of his career.

Rustin was also contemptuous of the black studies programs that began to appear on university campuses in the late 1960s and 1970s. As with affirmative action, his quarrel lay with the ways in which these programs diverted attention and resources from the central issue of poverty in America. Although he had rejected communism decades earlier, Rustin remained a materialist—one who believed that economics and class relations determined history. Although black studies courses might promote pride in identity and respect for one's culture, they could not feed the hungry or provide the training and preparation African Americans would need to acquire jobs in an increasingly technology-based economy.

Rustin did not shrink from delivering this message directly to young African Americans. In a 1968 speech at historically black Clark College in Atlanta, he cautioned students against "examining their navels when they should be examining economic and social programs." Black youth, he charged, "are more concerned with the way they wear their hair and whether or not they are called 'black' or 'Afro-American' than with developing strategies to solve the problems of housing, poverty and jobs."[5] In an article appearing in 1969, he described black studies as a "cheap separatist solution" that provided "psychic comfort for Negro student(s) only temporarily." They allowed colleges to avoid "the expenditure of hundreds of thousands of dollars for a larger teaching staff and for remedial efforts that will improve . . . (black) performance in mathematics, reading, and writing— skills that are useful in the real world."[6] Black studies programs taught African Americans to hold their heads high, but imparted no marketable skills.

Rustin also argued that these programs encouraged separatism and attitudes of racial superiority that served only to divide Americans from each other. "I am opposed," Rustin wrote in his 1969 article, "to the concept of black studies to the degree that it separates the contribution of black men from the study of American history and society. . . . A multiple society cannot exist where one element in that society, out of its own sense of guilt and masochism, permits any other element to hold a gun at its head in the name of justice."[7] Thus, at a moment when the value of black studies was becoming conventional wisdom in the African American community and on the left generally, Rustin had again positioned himself deliberately and forcefully against his former allies. By 1970, marginalized even further from these constituencies, he was being referred to as the "housenigger of the Democratic Party" by an ex-WRL colleague enraged by what he considered Rustin's racial accommodationism.[8] Speaking invitations from colleges would still come throughout the 1970s and 1980s, but fewer and fewer of them would be from those with substantial numbers of black students.

Rustin's stances on Israel, affirmative action, and black studies brought him closer to the right, but they did not make him a rightist. On class-related issues, he remained a committed socialist. Although aligned philosophically with Reagan administration positions on the conduct of the Cold War, he vehemently opposed its social service spending cuts, tax reductions, and attempts to shrink the role of the government in the national economy. From his base in the Randolph Institute, Rustin issued a steady stream of position papers and news releases attacking the economic policies of the Reagan administration, under which, he charged, "the poor have gotten poorer and the rich richer."[9] Reagan's "blind reliance on market forces and (his) belief that government has no role to play" in the struggle for economic equality in the United States, Rustin charged, had brought about "a reversal of a fifty year-long trend toward greater social justice."[10]

Even as Reaganomics took hold during the 1980s, Rustin continued to insist on the primacy of the federal government in the battle against poverty and want in America. If Reagan believed, as he often stated, that "government is the problem," Rustin never lost confidence in it as a solution, a powerful instrument of justice and deliverance.[11] Rustin had seen the federal government launch coordinated attacks on want in America through the New Deal and the War on Poverty, and on racial segregation through landmark civil rights legislation. He had also seen it take the lead in creating jobs for Americans through programs such as FDR's Works Progress Administration, which created a national infrastructure of roads, bridges, parks, and schools. In his mind, the work of the government was far from done.

Nor was the job of organized labor. Rustin spoke out on behalf of American workers at every opportunity during the last years of his life, again placing him at odds with a Reagan administration that was no friend of unions. A notable example of Rustin's continuing devotion to the cause of labor came in 1984, when he traveled to New Haven, Connecticut, to aid striking clerical employees at Yale University. Rustin had received an honorary degree from the school earlier that year, and it would not have been surprising had he shied away from a controversy involving a powerful institution with which he had established a relationship. But in a battle between a union struggling for recognition and an elite university, his choice was clear. Rustin demonstrated alongside the striking workers against the Yale administration and was among those arrested. It could not have been lost on him that many self-styled New Leftists on the Yale faculty sat on the sidelines during the strike, fearful of the harm that supporting the union might do to their careers. Throughout his life, Rustin was willing to make personal sacrifices for his beliefs in ways many of his critics were not. The Yale strike, near the end of that life, was emblematic.

Even as he fought for the rights of labor, Rustin sought to use the goodwill he had generated among union officials to induce them to provide openings for minorities in their industries. The skilled craft unions of the AFL-CIO were notoriously closed off to nonwhites. Union jobs as plumbers, electricians, carpenters, and welders, among others, were handed down from father to son, almost as a birthright. Rustin set out to change this long-standing practice and to strengthen the alliance between minorities and labor that was so dear to him. Through the Randolph Institute, he sponsored the Recruitment and Training Program (RTP), which placed young African Americans and Hispanics in apprentice positions with building trade unions, then gave them the background they needed to become full-time employees. Rustin obtained the cooperation of AFL-CIO President George Meany, as well as New York City Central Labor Council head Harry Van Arsdale, and was also able to coax federal funding for the program from the Nixon and Carter administrations. RTP did not succeed in transforming the racial practices of the building trades, which remained largely white-dominated. But it did bring thousands of minority youths into apprenticeships and increased their percentages in construction field unions by almost 20 percent between 1972 and 1976.[12]

RTP also avoided the government-imposed racial quotas of formal affirmative action programs, which Rustin opposed. Instead, the building trade unions acted voluntarily to reach out to minorities, offering access but no guarantee of success. Black and Hispanic applicants took the same examinations as their white counterparts, with no special set-asides. Although this arrangement did not satisfy civil rights leaders, including those in the NAACP, it reflected Rustin's conviction that true American equality was race-blind. His rejection of affirmative action was not a concession to the racism of the AFL-CIO unions that financed the Randolph Institute, as some charged, but an expression of his class-consciousness. No policy that divided the American working class, no matter how well meaning, could fulfill the nation's promise of full equality. Only more resources—for everyone—would.

By the 1980s many of Rustin's political allies were not radicals or even on the left, and the civil rights movement had written him off as a man of the past. But in his unceasing advocacy of the rights of working men and women, his faith in government as a vehicle of systemic change, his focus on poverty and jobs, and his demand for a fundamental redistribution of wealth and resources in the United States, Rustin remained committed to a radical agenda for the United States. He rejected capitalism both as an economic system and a set of values, offering in its place a transformative egalitarian vision. Unlike many Americans, he understood that the nation's founding documents—the Declaration of Independence and the Constitution—did not enshrine a particular economic philosophy. Instead, they articulated the principles of equality and freedom as goals for a democratic people. After a brief flirtation with communism as a young man, Rustin adopted socialism because he believed it embodied those principles and provided the means to achieve them. Through all the twists and turns of his political journey, from imprisoned war resister to presidential confidante, he never deviated from his position that socialism, and not capitalism, was the true American creed. Critics who charged that Rustin had "changed" over the years, that he had become a conservative or "establishment" figure, missed the point. His challenge to the nation's prevailing economic order was consistent, lifelong, and revolutionary.

Rustin had never viewed his homosexuality as anything more than a personal choice, with no political implications beyond those that caused damage to his professional career. This began to change in 1977, when he met Walter Naegle on a Manhattan street corner. Naegle was a white man in his late twenties, with some of the same pacifist sensibilities as Rustin. He had opposed the war in Vietnam as a college student, and chose alternative service working with the elderly when faced with induction into the military. Naegle was preparing to leave New York for San Francisco when Rustin struck up a chance conversation with him, but he soon abandoned this idea. Although Rustin was almost forty years older, the two men established a deep emotional connection, and within a year Naegle had moved into Rustin's apartment on West 28th Street. Naegle became both Rustin's romantic partner and his personal anchor. There had been many affairs in Rustin's past, but none gave him the sense of closeness and security that he craved. Now, nearing the end of his life, he had at last found a life partner. Thanks to Naegle, Rustin's last ten years were his happiest.

Naegle helped Rustin become more at ease with his sexual orientation. Rustin came of age at a time when homosexuality was only whispered about by "respectable" people—"Bayard's problem" was how his colleagues at FOR had described it. But Naegle was raised in a 1960s atmosphere that was much less judgmental and restrictive. He was comfortable with who he was, and that helped make Rustin more comfortable as well. Their relationship was "public" in ways Rustin's previous liaisons were not. Naegle accompanied Rustin on his humanitarian trips around the world and worked with him at the Randolph Institute. They made no attempt to disguise the fact that they were living together, socializing as freely as any "straight" couple. His relationship with Naegle helped Rustin undo much of the psychological damage of decades spent struggling with his conscience—not to mention the judgments of men like A. J. Muste and Martin Luther King, Jr.—regarding his sexual choices. Through the relaxed matter-of-factness of his days with Naegle, Rustin put a lifetime of personal turmoil to rest.

During his final years, Rustin incorporated the new attitude toward his sexuality that Naegle helped nurture into his politics. The homosexual rights

Rustin with Walter Naegle, 1980s. Source: Estate of
Bayard Rustin.

movement had begun in 1969 when a police raid on a Greenwich Village gay
bar, the Stonewall Inn, incited a violent reaction from patrons and their supporters in the surrounding neighborhood. Gays began defining themselves as a
distinct identity group in much the same manner as African Americans, Hispanics, and women. Like these groups, homosexuals worked for both legal and
social equality.

By the 1980s Rustin viewed gay rights as the logical extension of the civil
rights movement, and in many ways its culmination. He became active in the
campaign to amend New York City's human rights law to explicitly prohibit discrimination against homosexuals. In the process, he locked horns with a number of local black political officials, whose discomfort with homosexuality was
reminiscent of that of the civil rights leadership during the 1950s and 1960s.
The hypocrisy of those who opposed civil rights protections for gays while vigorously supporting them for African Americans was obvious, and Rustin did not
hesitate to point this out.

But he also framed his arguments in favor of extending the coverage of the
law in broader terms. Gays were the last American minority subjected to overt

discrimination in American society. They could be ridiculed publicly in ways that blacks, Hispanics, or Jews could not. Their lifestyles were considered illegal in many jurisdictions, a burden no other group had to bear. And with the advent of the acquired immunodeficiency syndrome (AIDS) crisis in the early 1980s, they were clearly "people in trouble." To Rustin, civil rights for homosexuals represented the fulfillment of the American dream of equality for all. He would have preferred that sexual orientation remain a private matter. But by criminalizing and stigmatizing homosexual behavior, American society itself had forced the issue and made personal choices public concerns. Gays were as worthy of protection, both under the law and in American society generally, as members of any other marginalized group.

Rustin did not see homosexuals as possessing an "identity" separate from that of other Americans. He was moved by their persecution and wished to see them recognized as first-class citizens. He worked for gays not because they were part of his family, but because they were part of the human family. Rustin lobbied city council members, testified at committee hearings, and spoke at rallies in support of a homosexual rights bill for New York, which was adopted in 1986 and became a model for cities across the nation. He continued to speak out on behalf of gay rights, always as part of a broader agenda of human rights, for the rest of his life.

During his last years, Rustin came to terms with himself both personally and politically. In the absence of domestic partnership laws in New York State, he adopted Naegle as his son so the younger man could remain in the apartment they shared after his death and inherit his assets. Randolph, his lifelong champion, died in 1979. Testifying at a congressional hearing when he received word, Rustin broke down and cried openly for a man who had never abandoned him.[13] He remained active in the Randolph Institute, taking special pleasure in its success of its campaigns to register African American voters and elect black public officials. The institute helped forge links between organized labor and the black community that would benefit the Democratic Party for decades to come. Rustin also served as leader of Social Democrats, USA, an offshoot of the Socialist Party, which had splintered in the 1970s. The group was an American version of the labor parties that had become so powerful during the twentieth century in Great Britain and across Europe. Rustin now understood that his dreams for socialism in the United States would not be fulfilled in his lifetime. The nation's politics were becoming increasingly conservative, and the momentum and promise of the 1960s had dissipated. But age and experience had afforded him a degree of equanimity in the face of political disappointment. He neither railed at circumstances nor his remaining critics. Time and history would be his judge.

Rustin suffered a heart attack in 1971 but recovered fully and remained vigorous well into the 1980s. In July 1987 he and Naegle traveled to Haiti on a

Freedom House–sponsored mission to promote democracy in that embattled nation. While there, he contracted an intestinal disorder, which persisted on his return to the United States. Doctors were unable to diagnose it with specificity, as he grew weaker and weaker. He was finally admitted to the hospital on August 21. Surgeons discovered a burst appendix accompanied by peritonitis, an inflammation of the abdomen. He underwent an operation, which appeared to succeed, and his condition stabilized briefly. But two days later, he lapsed into delirium. Alerted at home, Naegle raced to the hospital. Administrators refused to allow him into Rustin's room despite his legal status as his son. He waited in the hall as Rustin died of heart failure early in the morning of August 24, 1987, at the age of seventy-five.

Notes

1. Rustin died before the 1989 fall of the Berlin Wall, and the collapse of the Soviet Union in 1991 disproved his idea that Marxist states were incapable of change.

2. "Affirmative Action in an Economy of Scarcity," Testimony of Bayard Rustin, executive director, A. Philip Randolph Institute, and Norman Hill, associate director, A. Philip Randolph Institute, to the Special Subcommittee on Education, U.S. House of Representatives, September 17, 1974, Bayard Rustin Papers, Library of Congress, Washington, DC (hereinafter "Rustin Papers"), Reel 17, Frames 816–17.

3. Rustin Papers, Reel 17, Frame 809.

4. See Daniel Levine, *Bayard Rustin and the Civil Rights Movement* (New Brunswick, NJ: Rutgers University Press, 2000), pp. 221–23.

5. Bayard Rustin, Convocation Address, Clark College, Atlanta, Georgia, March 5, 1968, Rustin Papers, Reel 17, Frame 837.

6. Bayard Rustin, "Black Studies and Inequality," *Hotel-Bar-Restaurant Review*, June 1969, Rustin Papers, Reel 17, Frame 889.

7. Rustin Papers, "Black Studies and Inequality," Reel 17, Frame 889.

8. Letter, Jim Peck to Bayard Rustin, July 22, 1970, Rustin Papers, Reel 14, Frame 617.

9. Bayard Rustin, "The Poor Get Poorer," A. Philip Randolph Institute Release, August 23, 1984, Rustin Papers, Reel 19, Frame 1135.

10. Bayard Rustin, "Mitterrand and Reagan: A Study in Contrasts," A. Philip Randolph Institute Release, March 11, 1982, Rustin Papers, Reel 19, Frame 1091; Bayard Rustin, "Ronald Reagan and the Idea of Equality," A. Philip Randolph Institute Release, January 6, 1983, Rustin Papers, Reel 19, Frame 1116.

11. Ronald Reagan, Inaugural Address, January 20, 1981, *Public Papers of the Presidents of the United States, Ronald Reagan, January 20 to December 31, 1981* (Washington, DC: U.S. Government Printing Office, 1982), p. 1.

12. Levine, *Bayard Rustin and the Civil Rights Movement*, pp. 222–23.

13. See Andrew E. Kersten, A. *Philip Randolph: A Life in the Vanguard* (Lanham, MD: Rowman & Littlefield, 2007), p. 111.

~

Rustin's American Dreams

Death softened the hard edges of Rustin's critics. For days afterward, and at his memorial service on October 1, 1987, at New York's Community Church, words of praise and respect poured in. He was lauded as a visionary and a tireless fighter for justice. Representatives from all of his "lives"—pacifist, socialist, labor champion, civil rights activist, humanist—were present. The very multiplicity of these lives, however, made it difficult for any one tribute to capture him fully. Rustin was a man of great personal complexity. He rarely revealed all of who he was at once. Walter Naegle knew him best. Rustin walled off parts of himself from everyone else. Some of this was self-invention. Rustin's accent, for example, led many to assume he was of British or West Indian descent. He implied that he had been a full-time student at City College, when he had taken only a handful of night courses there. Rustin consciously cultivated an air of mystery about his origins and background.

But much of his guardedness came by necessity. Throughout his life, Rustin would sing the spiritual "Sometimes I Feel Like a Motherless Child" with great emotion. The song was especially meaningful to him because it captured the sadness and loneliness that accompanied a life wracked by intense insecurity. Rustin's relationship with his mother was fleeting. He barely knew his father. His grandparents were attentive and kind, but could not protect him after he left West Chester. Once out in the world, his existence was precarious and uncertain. Lacking a loving father, he sought substitutes in A. J. Muste and A. Philip Randolph. He did not earn what could be considered a decent income until he was in his fifties, and did not have an emotionally satisfying personal life until his sixties. He spent time in prison. He also lived as a black man when a word, a gesture, or a facial expression could carry severe consequences. And even some of his closest political allies could not accept his homosexuality.

Often it seemed that Rustin's life was at a dead end. He left two colleges without graduating. He refused to fight in the nation's most popular war. He was subjected to the indignities of a Southern chain gang. He was estranged at various times from Muste, Randolph, and Martin Luther King, Jr. He was convicted of a "morals" offense and lost his career at the Fellowship of Reconciliation. Rustin was able to survive these trials and more. But his tribulations made him fear that what he had might be taken from him, and he responded by dividing his life into compartments for his own protection. To some degree, then, he was hidden from virtually everyone who came to honor him at the Community Church that day in October 1987.

But even if the mourners had been familiar with all the parts of Rustin's life, he was greater than the sum of them. His political vision for the nation fit together in ways that his personal life did not. Rustin's American dream was broad and deep. He integrated his passions—civil rights, labor, socialism, democracy, peace—into an agenda that may have been unique in the annals of American radicalism for its coherence and logic. He fought for the rights of African Americans not only because their cause was just, but because their struggles overlapped with those of workers, the poor, pacifists, and homosexuals. Rustin sought to help "people in trouble" because he dreamed of a nation without economic, racial, and social barriers.

Rustin reading Gandhian philosophy, 1979. Source: Estate of Bayard Rustin.

Other American radicals also dreamed of equality and freedom, of course. But some, like Malcolm X, cast their dreams narrowly, seeking equality and freedom for "their" people only. Others, like Muste, could not make homosexuals part of their dreams. Even King's vision was limited by race. Although he spoke of an America without racial divisions at the March on Washington, by the time of his death in 1968 he had endorsed affirmative action as a remedy for past injustices and was doing little to prevent the Poor People's Campaign from becoming almost exclusively African American in composition. But when Rustin dreamed of an America in which all people were equal and free, he meant just that. He sought to help groups other than his own, and supported whites against blacks when, as at Ocean Hill-Brownsville, he believed right was on their side. To him, the civil rights movement was not a means to attain group power, but to make all Americans equal.

Moreover, unlike many radicals, Rustin developed a concrete program to achieve his dream. Since he understood that true equality was impossible in a nation with wide disparities in wealth, economic justice was the centerpiece of his agenda. Rustin argued that racism in America was rooted in class rivalries and resentments. Guaranteeing every American a job, an income, a good education, decent housing, and affordable medical care would address class-based jealousies that often were expressed in racial terms. Rustin was realistic enough to know that some racism was so deeply inbred as to be unaffected by economic conditions. But he was also idealistic enough to believe that providing for the material well-being of all would allow Americans to view one another as individuals and not through the prism of race. It is possible, of course, that Rustin was too optimistic in this regard. As the decades following the March on Washington showed, when the imperatives of class ran up against those of race, the latter usually won out. It was these ongoing racial animosities in the 1960s and 1970s that largely eclipsed economic concerns and made it impossible for Rustin to build a constituency for his program. He regarded these impediments to interracial solidarity, however, as temporary. Eventually Americans would see that their true interests lay with one another.

This optimism explains why, in contrast to many revolutionaries, Rustin trusted democracy so deeply. He had confidence in the judgments of average men and women. Many radicals, especially those affiliated with the New Left, professed to have faith in "the people," but reacted contemptuously when they did not behave as they wished. Rustin, who had spent considerably more time among "the people" than the average New Leftist, never did. To him, they were not an abstraction, but intensely human, and as such capable of defining and pursuing their own interests. As much as he desired socialism in the United States, he would not accept it being imposed from above by self-appointed tribunes of "the people." If it could not come about through democratic processes, Rustin did not want it at all.

Related to his devotion to democracy was Rustin's belief in nonviolence as a strategy and philosophy. Nonviolent direct action was by its nature democratic, for it gave voice to those who could not otherwise speak. It was a pure expression of the popular will. Rustin probably envisioned a less prominent role for civil disobedience in the inclusive, socially democratic nation of his dreams. A society in which every individual had value—where material needs were satisfied and all were truly equal under the law—would provide avenues for protest and redress of grievances in most instances. But Rustin believed that there should always be space for expressions of personal conscience, and that the availability of civil disobedience to those who needed it was a sign of a society that was still capable of growth and change.

Rustin's radical program, finally, was uncompromisingly integrationist. His former allies on the left and in the civil rights movement lost faith in interracialism, but Rustin did not. No nation that was segregated, whether by law, custom, or choice, could ever be just. Rustin opposed any policy, no matter how well intentioned, that separated Americans by race. This, more than anything else, explains his discomfort with affirmative action and community control of education. He would have opposed all-black academies or school programs in the twenty-first century for the same reason. It also explains why coalition politics became so important to him during the last twenty-five years of his life. Rustin did not reject racial identity, or group identity, out of hand. He was, of course, proud of his own African American heritage. But he could never accept an America in which racial identity was the primary referent, and where blacks and whites lived in different geographic, political, and cultural worlds. Of all the components of Rustin's dream, integration may have been the least attainable, but he refused to let go of it. A racially segregated American nation could never be true to itself.

Economic justice. Democracy. Nonviolence. Interracialism. The elements of Rustin's American dream were interconnected. They fit together as a program, a specific plan for achieving equality and freedom in the United States. Most American radicals spoke of these goals. Rustin was one of the very few to offer a road map with which to get there.

Rustin did not leave the United States as he found it. His introduction to Martin Luther King, Jr., during the Montgomery bus boycott in 1956 changed American history. Rustin had immersed himself in the practice and ideology of nonviolent direct action for decades before he met King, but was still a marginal figure. King stood on the threshold of a racial revolution in America as the public voice of the Montgomery boycott, but possessed only a vague sense of the direction in which it should go. Thanks to Rustin, nonviolent direct action gave the nascent civil rights movement both a practical strategy and its moral power, allowing African Americans to break down a century-old edifice of political and social oppression.

Without Rustin's understanding of nonviolent direct action's potential and his ability to communicate it to King, the Jim Crow South may have remained locked in time. Without Rustin's organizational skills, the March on Washington would not have become, as it did, the defining moment of the civil rights movement. Rustin did not write the words of the "I Have a Dream" speech, but without his guidance, it is doubtful King would have been in a position to utter them on August 28, 1963. Rustin was as responsible for the Civil Rights Act of 1964 and the Voting Rights Act of 1965 as any American, black or white. He helped to effect the most far-reaching political and social transformation of the twentieth century in the United States. The rise of a substantial black middle class, the emergence of African American voters as the "base" of the Democratic Party, and the election of thousands of black public officials, all a direct result of Rustin's efforts, testify to the magnitude of the revolution he did so much to initiate.

At the same time, Rustin's life illustrated the limits of the radical impulse in the United States. Many of his dreams for America did not come true. The interracial alliance between the labor and civil rights movements that he envisioned was unsustainable. Even unions like the United Auto Workers and United Federation of Teachers, which had supported the work of Martin Luther King, Jr., and whose leaders had been prominent at the March on Washington, clashed with the African American community. In virtually every such confrontation, white and black workers identified by race first and as workers second. Rustin looked to a day when such a choice would no longer be necessary, but he did not live to see it. Indeed, he was himself forced into an awful choice between class and racial allegiances at Ocean Hill-Brownsville in 1968. Unions were the linchpins of Rustin's American dream. Labor's inability to forge an enduring partnership with African Americans may have been his greatest disappointment.

America's failure to embrace democratic socialism was another disappointment. After the triumph of the March on Washington, Rustin had hoped that the moment for socialism might be at hand. The Freedom Budget of 1966 was the concrete expression of that hope. But it was not to be. Although it was true that the Freedom Budget sank under the weight of Vietnam War–related turmoil on the left, it failed as well to gain traction with the American public at large. The 1960s ended, in fact, with confidence ebbing in government's ability to alleviate poverty in the United States. Many Americans viewed the War on Poverty, which Rustin did not believe went far enough, as a failure. By the 1980s, conservative Ronald Reagan was telling appreciative national audiences that "the Government declared a war on poverty. Poverty won."[1] When in 1996 Bill Clinton said "the era of big government is over," and signed legislation that effectively terminated the federal public assistance program with the words "we are ending welfare as we know it," he was signaling the mainstream Democratic Party's rejection of Rustin's socialist agenda.[2]

In 1906 the sociologist Werner Sombart asked famously, "Why is there no socialism in the United States?"[3] His question hung unanswered over American political life throughout the twentieth century and into the twenty-first. There have been instances of intense antibusiness and even anticapitalist sentiment in the United States, notably during the New Deal and the decade of the 1960s. But alongside this egalitarian impulse ran another cultural strain, which was deeply individualist in character and hostile to the idea of government-sponsored redistribution of resources in American society. Rustin was aware of this strain and sought to sidestep it during his campaign for the Freedom Budget by arguing that the federal government could guarantee a job, an income, and medical care to every American without raising taxes, reducing military spending, or overregulating the economy. That even with these assurances Rustin was unable to assemble a national constituency for the Freedom Budget at a time when the War on Poverty was already under way illustrated the difficulties socialists faced in convincing the American people to cede a measure of their economic freedom to the federal government.

Rustin struggled his entire life against a capitalist culture that celebrated individualism and competition. Replacing this culture with one based on cooperation and mutual obligation proved to be a battle he could not win. His socialist creed, in fact, trapped him between two great American ideals. Rustin dreamed of a nation where all were judged on their merits and given the opportunity to rise to the level of their individual talents. At the same time, he sought an America in which all were entitled to an equal share of the nation's resources, and where under certain conditions individuals might be required to give up part of what they had earned for the benefit of the community as a whole. This tension between the individual and the community has been a persistent theme throughout American history, and Rustin could not be expected to resolve it on his own. But as a socialist, he was particularly vulnerable to the contradictions inherent in a nation that aspires to both freedom and equality, and his program, including the Freedom Budget, fell victim to them.

If Rustin's life exemplified the limits of American radicalism, it also illustrated those of coalition politics. Although his years as a radical "outsider" were marked by marginalization and ineffectuality, they at least offered the consolation of moral purity. The time he spent as a Democratic Party "insider" in the years following the March on Washington, during which he enjoyed access to the highest levels of "establishment" political power, was painful in a different way. It forced him to make compromises—on the war in Vietnam, at the Atlantic City Democratic Convention, during the Ocean Hill-Brownsville crisis—in the hope of effecting tangible change through a coalition of mainstream

Democrats, African Americans, church members, liberals, socialists, and labor unions. But Rustin's dream failed to take shape. Its component parts crashed against one another and broke away. Labor clashed with the black community over the meaning of racial equality. Democratic politicians broke with African Americans, religious leaders, and the liberal wing of their own party over issues of war and peace. Labor and the Democratic leadership disagreed over the extent of the federal government's role in ending poverty and ensuring that every American had an income, a job, and adequate health care.

As things fell apart, Rustin was caught in the wreckage. His efforts at coalition and compromise earned him only scorn from those who had come to view him as unprincipled and morally corrupted. Sellout. Hypocrite. Warmonger. Uncle Tom. The rewards of national prominence could not compensate Rustin for the wounds inflicted by former allies and colleagues outraged by what they considered his devil's bargain. Rustin's experiences in coalition politics proved that the life of an "insider" could be just as fraught with disappointment as that of a shadow man. Like the components of the coalition he sought to assemble during the 1960s, the constituents of Rustin's American dream pushed against one another throughout his life and career. On one level this bears witness to the expansive nature of that dream. Rustin pressed an agenda for an America in which material needs were satisfied, marginalized groups enjoyed full equality, the economy was managed by the government for the good of all, and nonviolence was a national principle. He pursued socialism, pacifism, racial equality, and civil rights simultaneously, an ambitious undertaking to say the least.

But the ways in which the aspects of Rustin's dream clashed also speak to the constraints of American radicalism in twentieth-century America and serve as a caution to those who dream of such a movement in the twenty-first. Rustin's ambitions forced him into difficult choices—Marxism against racial equality in 1941, when the American Communist Party ordered a moratorium on civil rights activity; pacifism against civil rights in 1948 during the campaign to desegregate the military; peace against socialism in 1966 as he worked for the adoption of the Freedom Budget. In these and other instances, Rustin made his choices and struggled to hold the pieces of his dream together. Finally, during the Ocean Hill-Brownsville crisis in 1968, he faced a choice that was not merely difficult but impossible, as civil and labor rights collided in a manner that forced him to turn his back on one of them. He would not recover from this clash of dreams. Of all his colliding imperatives, those of class and race were the most toxic, as the events at Ocean Hill-Brownsville showed so poignantly. Reconciling them was beyond his ability. No radical agenda—Rustin's or any other—can hope to succeed in the United States until it does.

Rustin's America built on the dreams of Jefferson, Thoreau, Lincoln, Whitman, Du Bois, and Debs. The nation of his imagination was one in which all were not only created equal but also entitled to economic security. It was an open and inclusive democracy that valued both the individual and the individual conscience. And it was a nation in which men and women of all races, religions, ethnicities, and sexual orientations were free to be who they were and be American at the same time, judged ultimately not on their particularities but on their human qualities. Rustin's American dream, like those of his predecessors, remains a work in progress. There are still extremes of poverty and wealth in the United States. It is one of the most militarized societies in the world. African Americans and homosexuals, among others, continue to face formidable barriers to achieving their own American dreams. But the United States is nonetheless better for Rustin having lived in it. And like the six men who inspired him, Rustin ennobled America through the moral power of his dream. It remains a unique vision of equality and freedom that represents the best of what this nation offers its citizens and the world. Bayard Rustin's legacies are that dream and his ongoing challenge to realize it.

Notes

1. Ronald Reagan, "Remarks at Annual Dinner of the Knights of Malta," January 13, 1989, *Public Papers of the Presidents of the United States, Ronald Reagan, July 8, 1988 to January 19, 1989* (Washington, DC: U.S. Government Printing Office, 1991), p. 1734.

2. William J. Clinton, "Address Before a Joint Session of Congress on the State of the Union," January 23, 1996, *Public Papers of the Presidents of the United States, William J. Clinton, January 1 to June 30, 1996* (Washington, DC: U.S. Government Printing Office, 1997), p. 79; Francis X. Clines, "Clinton Signs Bill Cutting Welfare," *New York Times*, August 23, 1996, pp. A1, A22.

3. See Werner Sombart, *Why Is There No Socialism in the United States?* (White Plains, NY: International Arts and Sciences Press, 1976).

~

Documents

"Interracial Primer" (1943)

Rustin wrote the following introduction to a Fellowship of Reconciliation (FOR) pamphlet on interracial organizing for political, social, and economic justice.

The Negro in 1943

In the past two years several encouraging developments have occurred in the American Negro-white scene. President Roosevelt has issued Executive Order 8802, clearly forbidding discrimination in war industries because of race, color, creed, or national origin. A new and more powerful Fair Employment Practices Committee has been set up. The major labor organizations have taken a fairly progressive stand, and encourage member unions to be diligent in applying their National Councils' resolutions on equity. And Americans generally have displayed increased concern about the undemocratic conditions against which Negroes must contend.

Nevertheless, in spite of these developments, Negro-white tension has increased steadily since the United States entered the war. . . .

Thus, as the American Negro at last takes the offensive in his struggle for freedom, he is confronted by organized violence, and must overcome an increased separation from the white world, and consequently from political power and self-government. . . .

Denied jobs, housing, and education, thousands of Negroes literally are starving to death in a nation that at the same time conscripts other black men and asks them to kill and to die for democracy. . . .

It is tragic also how isolated the Negro feels in his struggle. The average Negro largely has lost faith in middle-class whites. He believes that his insistence on liberty has drawn a clear line between black and white. He believes that the vanguard of the old order would rather see fascism come to America than liberty to the Negro. It is not Japanese propaganda that creates this feeling, but the very nature of our economic, social, and political life. In his hour of need the Negro seeks not talk but dynamic action. He looks upon the middle-class idea of long-term educational and cultural changes with fear and mistrust when they are not accompanied by action.

The average Negro is interested primarily in how he can get jobs, decent housing, and education for his children. He describes with disgust the efforts on his behalf by most middle-class Negro and white intellectuals as "pink tea methods—sometimes well-meanin' but getting' us nowhere." For this reason some Negroes have tended to black nationalism. The black nationalist says, "These are the Negro's problems and nobody but the Negro is really anxious to solve them. So let's organize black." One of the newer and most militant Negro organizations voted last fall to reject white people in both constituency and leadership.

If present irritating conditions continue, before long we surely shall see race riots, if not during the war then after. We shall see them in Northern industrial cities and in rural and urban sections of the South. For Negroes no longer will continue to accept second-class citizenship.

Those of us who believe in the principles of brotherhood have before us a terrible responsibility to do all in our power to stop this trend to violence and to create interracial good will by giving of our time, energy, and money to remove from our local communities the conditions that maintain injustice and exploitation and that lead to bitterness and aggression.

*   *   *

"Lecture and Discussion— Saturday Afternoon, October 9, 1943"

Rustin's notes for a workshop he conducted in California on nonviolent social change.

The philosophies of violence and non-violence see the nature of truth from two different points of view. Violence insists that it has the truth and that anything different is a lie. It maintains that things which are diametrically opposed cannot be reconciled. Men holding opposing ideas must be opposed to each other, because men cannot be separated from the things they believe.

The non-violent philosophy claims that we are all incapable of seeing the truth. Each of us sees part of the truth because each of us looks at truth from a different point of view. This makes conflict inevitable, it is undeniable. We cannot say easily, "Here comes reconciliation. How nice! Let's shake hands and smile." Conflict means struggle and the point is whether it will be solved violently or non-violently. Our own views of truth are conditioned by the environment in which we have been exposed. If someone else seems to us to hold a wrong point of view, we must stand before that person so that we are examples of the truth and may make him see a new level of thinking. But we cannot force our view upon him. . . .

Non-violence has three aims as it participates in a struggle: to gain the respect and sympathy of the other party, to gain the support of the public, and finally to achieve progress. The first two are concerned with means, the third with ends. Violent struggle is concerned only with ends. If it is at all concerned with means, these points can be attended to only after the struggle is over, while in the non-violent method they are of primary importance. . . .

The step of non-violent direct action is the use of the only real weapons left to a man, his body and his soul-force, the force of his convictions, "casting his total vote," as Thoreau says. Discipline is very important at this point, but it must never be discipline for its own sake. Discipline comes as the situation demands. Learning comes by doing. It is very important, in this connection, that one cannot separate oneself from the masses and then come back and hope to understand them and be accepted by them as a leader. True understanding comes only as one is a part of the masses and acts with them. . . .

*   *   *

Letter to Draft Board, November 16, 1943

After he received his military induction notice, Rustin wrote the following letter to his draft board.

974 St. Nicholas Avenue
New York, N.Y.
November 16, 1943

Local Board No. 63
2050 Amsterdam Avenue
New York, N.Y.

Gentlemen:

For eight years I have believed war to be impractical and a denial of our Hebrew Christian tradition. The social teachings of Jesus are: (1) Respect for personality; (2) Service . . .; (3) Overcoming evil with good; and (4) The brotherhood of man. These principles as I see it are violated by participation in war.

Believing this, and having before me Jesus' continued resistance to that which he considered evil, I was compelled to resist war by registering as a Conscientious Objector in October, 1940.

However, a year later, September 1941, I became convinced that conscription as well as war equally is inconsistent with the teachings of Jesus. I must resist conscription also.

On Saturday, November 13, 1943, I received from you an order to report for a physical examination to be taken Tuesday, November 16 at eight o'clock in the evening. I wish to inform you that I cannot voluntarily submit to an order springing from the Selective Service and Training Act for War.

There are several reasons for this decision, all stemming from the basic spiritual truth that men are brothers in the sight of God:

(1) War is wrong. Conscription is a concomitant of modern war. Thus conscription for so vast an evil as war is wrong.

(2) Conscription for war is inconsistent with freedom of conscience, which is not merely the right to believe, but to act on the degree of truth that one receives, to follow a vocation which is God-inspired and God-directed.

Today I feel that God motivates me to use my whole being to combat by non-violent means the ever-growing racial tension in the United States; at the same time the State directs that I shall do its will; which of these dictates can I follow—that of God or that of the State? Surely, I must at all times attempt to obey the law of the State. But when the will of God and the will of the State conflict, I am compelled to follow the will of God. If I cannot continue in my present vocation, I must resist.

(3) The Conscription Act denies brotherhood—most basic New Testament teaching. Its design and purpose is to set men apart—German against American, American against Japanese. Its aim springs from a moral impossibility—that ends justify means, that from unfriendly acts a new and friendly world can emerge.

In practice further, it separates black from white—those supposedly struggling for a common freedom. Such a separation also is based on the moral error that racism can overcome racism, that evil can produce good, that men virtually in slavery can struggle for a freedom they are denied. This means that I must protest racial discrimination in the armed forces, which is not only morally indefensible but also in clear violation of the Act. This does not, however, imply that I could have a part in conforming to the Act if discrimination were eliminated. . . .

I admit my share of guilt for having participated in the institutions and ways of life which helped bring fascism and war. Nonetheless, guilty as I am, I now see as did the Prodigal Son that it is never too late to refuse longer to remain in a non-creative situation. It is always timely and virtuous to change—to take in all humility a new path.

Though joyfully following the will of God, I regret that I must break the law of the State. I am prepared for whatever may follow. . . .

Sincerely yours,

Bayard Rustin

* * *

Excerpts of Letter from Rustin to Doris Grotewohl, May 5, 1944

Rustin wrote his friend Doris Grotewohl of his attempt to integrate Ashland Federal Penitentiary through nonviolent direct action.

May 5, 1944

. . . Recently we worked with the administration to achieve a major change in policy—mixing racially in the common or recreation rooms. . . . Of course, there was great timidity on the part of the Negroes to go freely into the new situation as there had been several threats of violence as the result of the progressive move. . . . Well, on last Sunday (amid twilight and uncertainty) several men (all member of F.O.R.) went into the area. . . . To the man, blow after blow, all stood without "violence in word or deed". . . . And the power of it? The maintenance of non-violence did several things: (1) served as an example to all of the power of non-violence, (2) placed us in a position where we could ask the administration to maintain a firm and progressive position, (3) raised the C.O. in the minds of inmates, guards, etc., particularly in that 'we took it' but refused to allow punishment to the user of violence, (4) revealed to the Negroes involved that progress is possible only if non-violence is used (for certainly in this case, one violent word or act on our part would have meant defeat in ever so many ways).

* * *

"General Observations on the Journey of Reconciliation" (1947)

In this report to FOR and the Congress of Racial Equality, Rustin described responses to the Journey of Reconciliation's campaign to integrate public transportation facilities in the South.

Confusion
The one word which most universally describes the attitude of police, of passengers and of the Negro and white bus riders is "confusion". This state resulted from the fact that these various groups taking part in the psychological struggle in the buses and trains either did not know of the Morgan decision or, if they did, possessed no clear understanding of it. Thus when police officers and bus drivers in authority took a stand, they tended to act on the basis of what they knew – the state Jim Crow law. In the South, where the caste system is rigidly defined, this confusion is extremely dangerous, and leads to frustration. Frustration is usually followed by aggression in some form. . . .

Absence of Violence in Bus
In all the experiments there was not one overt act of violence on the part of anyone in the buses. The most extreme negative reactions were verbal, but without profanity. Typical of this is the statement of a young Marine who said: "The K.K.K. is coming up again and I guess I'll join up." The one act of violence against a member of the group was on the part of a taxi cab driver outside the bus station at Chapel Hill. This act – a single but hard blow to the head – was directed against a white man.

Uncle Tom Reaction
On three occasions when Negro testers protested discrimination by sitting in the front, other Negroes – a porter, a school teacher, and a day laborer – urged the resisters in very emotional terms to comply with the law. Their request was in part the result of fear, or as in the case of the Negro porter, an attempt to ingratiate himself with the white authorities. Such reactions are to be expected in a caste system and represent the kind of personal degradation which ought to spur us on to eliminate caste. . . .

Non-Violence
Without exception those arrested behaved in a non-violent fashion. They acted without fear, spoke quietly and firmly, showing great consideration for the police and bus drivers, and repeatedly pointed to the fact that they expected the police to do their duty as they saw it. We can not overemphasize the necessity for this courteous and intelligent manner while breaking with the caste system. It is our belief that the reason the police behaved politely stems from the fact that there was not the slightest provocation in the attitude of the resisters. On the other hand, we tried at all times to understand their attitude and position first.

Interracial Group a Necessity
Another reason for the lack of tension was the result of the group's being interracial. We did not allow a single situation to develop so that the struggle ap-

peared to be between white and Negro persons, but rather that progressives and democrats, white and black, were working by peaceful means to overcome a system which they felt to be wrong.

Necessity for Southerners
More and more we became aware that the more Southern people who refused to accept Jim Crow the better. If a small portion of the white population refused Jim Crow, as now practiced it would be impossible. There is a resentment against Northerners, who are considered plants and imports. Our trip would have been reduced greatly in effectiveness had there not been a number of people along who were born in the south, and some who are now living there. . . .

Direct Action
It is our belief that without direct action on the part of groups and individuals, the Jim Crow pattern in the south can not be broken down. We are equally certain that such direct action must be non-violent.

The Importance of Women
Generally it appears that the women were more intellectually inquisitive, open for discussion, and liberal in their sentiments than men. On several occasions women not only defended those who broke with Jim Crow, but gave their names and addresses offering to act as witnesses. One might then conclude that in appealing for aid (in the psychological struggle within the bus) one might do well to concentrate on winning over women. . . .

People Prepared for Change
We believe that the great majority of the people in the upper South are prepared to accept the Irene Morgan decision and to ride on buses and trains with Negroes. One white woman, reluctantly taking a seat beside a Negro man, said to her sister who was about to protest that she should take care: "I'm tired. Anything for a seat.". . .

Flux
The situation in the upper south is in a great state of flux. The indication is that where numerous cases have been brought, that is to say, where there has been great resistance, as in northern Virginia, the barriers are already down, and Negroes can, in large part, ride without fear of arrest. However, there are other parts of Virginia where there are repeated arrests. This picture of Virginia is in part true for North Carolina, eastern Tennessee, and Kentucky. One has reason to believe that when in the other areas there has been as much a concentrated educational effort and non-violent resistance as has occurred in upper Virginia, conditions will equally improve.

*   *   *

"A Report on Twenty-Two Days on the Chain Gang at Roxboro, North Carolina" (1949)

Here Rustin recounted his brutal chain gang experiences as he served his sentence for violating segregation laws during the Journey of Reconciliation.

I started from the camp for my first day's work on the road with anything but an easy mind. Our crew of 15 men was met at the back gate by the walking boss, who directed the day's work, and by a guard who carried both a revolver and a shotgun. We were herded into the rear of a truck where we were under constant scrutiny by the armed guard; who rode in a small glass-enclosed trailer behind. In that way we rode each day to whatever part of Persons County we were to work in. We would leave the truck when we were ordered to. At all times we had to be within sight of the guard, but at no time closer than thirty feet to him.

On this first day I got down from the truck with the rest of the crew. There were several moments of complete silence that seemed to leave everyone uneasy. Then the walking boss, whom I shall call Captain Jones, looked directly at me.

"Hey you, tall boy! How much time you got?"

"Thirty days, " I said politely.

"Thirty days, *Sir.*"

"Thirty days, Sir," I said.

He took a newsclipping from his pocket and waved it up and down.

"You're the one who thinks he's smart. Ain't got no respect. Tries to be uppity. Well, we'll learn you. You'll learn that you got to respect us down here. You ain't in Yankeeland now. We don't like no Yankee ways.". . .

I had never handled a pick in my life, but I tried. Captain Jones watched me sardonically for a few minutes. Then he grabbed the pick from me, raised it over his head and sank it deep into the earth several times.

"There now," he shouted, "let's see you do it."

I took the pick and tried to duplicate his method and his vigor. For about ten minutes I succeeded in breaking the ground. My arms and back began to give out, but I was determined to continue. Just as I was beginning to feel faint, a chain-ganger called "Purple" walked over to me and said quietly, "O.K. Let me are dat pick for a while. You take the shovel and no matter what they say or do, keep workin', keep tryin' and keep yo' mouth shut."

I took the shovel and began to throw the loose dirt into the truck. My arms pained so badly that for a while I thought each shovelful would be the last. . . .

As Purple walked over and began to pick again he whispered to me, "Now you'se learnin'. Sometimes you'll give out, but you can't never give up –dat's chain-gangin'!"

But I still had much "learnin'" to do. An hour later we moved to another job. As I sat in the truck I racked my mind for some way to convince Captain Jones that I was not "uppity" and yet at the same time to maintain self-respect. I hit upon two ideas. I should try to work more willingly and harder than anyone in the crew, and I should be as polite and as considerate of all persons in our small prison community as possible.

When the truck stopped and we were ordered out I made an effort to carry through my resolution by beginning work immediately. In my haste, I came within twenty feet of the guard.

"Stop you bastard!" he screamed, and pointed his revolver squarely toward my head. "Git back, git back. Don't rush me or I'll shoot the goddamned life out of you.". . .

Just after lunch we had begun to do what the chain-gangers call 'jumpin' shoulders' which means cutting the top from the shoulders of the road when they have grown too high. Usually the crew works with two trucks. There is scarcely a moment of delay and the work is extremely hard. Captain Jones was displeased with the rate of our work, and violently urged us to greater effort. In an effort to obey one of the chain-gangers struck another with his shovel. The victim complained, instantly and profanely. The words were hardly out of his mouth before the Captain stroked across the road and struck the cursing chain-ganger in the face with his fist, again and again. Then, as everyone watched apprehensively, Captain Jones informed the crew, using the most violent profanity in doing so, that cursing would not be tolerated!

"Not for one goddamned moment," he repeated over and over again.

No one spoke; every man tried to work harder yet remain inconspicuous. The silence seemed to infuriate the Captain. He glared angrily at the toiling men, than yelled to the armed guard.

"Shoot hell out of the next one you find cursin'. Shoot straight for his feet. Cripple 'em up. That will learn 'em."

The guard lifted his rifle and aimed it at the chest of the man nearest him.

"Hell, no!" he drawled, "I ain't aimin' fer no feet. I like hearts and livers. That's what really learns 'em."

Everyone spaded faster.

*　　*　　*

Announcement of Rustin's "Morals" Conviction and Termination From Fellowship of Reconciliation (1953)

A.J. Muste, FOR leader and Rustin's mentor, viewed his homosexuality as immoral, and fired him after he pleaded guilty to engaging in "lewd" activity with

two men in Pasadena, California. Muste announced his decision to the staff of
FOR in this memorandum.

To our great sorrow Bayard Rustin was convicted on a "morals charge" (homosexual) and sentenced to 60 days in the Los Angeles County Jail on January 23,
1953. As of that date his service as on F.O.R. staff member terminated.

That there was a problem in this field did not become known until after Bayard had been on the F.O.R. staff (which he joined in 1941) for some time. The
problem was seriously aggravated during his wartime prison experience.

From the very nature of the Fellowship it seemed to follow that there was no
simple way to deal with this problem. The course taken was to provide him with
counsel and help to deal with his problem, both for his own sake and in order
that his exceptional gifts might continue to be used in the cause to which he
was so deeply devoted. At the same time there was no disposition to minimize
the problem, and it was made clear that on his part continuance on the staff involved the exercise of rigorous discipline so that his work would not be affected
nor the movement compromised and so that his witness would increasingly be
purified and strengthened.

For some years, until the unhappy recent event, the situation seemed to be
moving along these lines. From many sources unsolicited testimony came, in
connection with his work for F.O.R. and A.F.S.C., that Bayard was growing spir-
itually as well as intellectually and proving a powerful exponent of non-violence. When questions were raised, as happened from time to time, the Staff
carefully investigated and in each case reported to it found that it referred to an
earlier period and not to recent years. Those who made such inquiries were ap-
prised of the situation. . . .

We are grateful to Bayard for the many services he has rendered, and sorrow
with him over the fact that he is not able to continue as an F.O.R. staff member. Our thoughts and prayers are with him.

*   *   *

"Statement on the Pacifist Demonstration in Connection With the June 15 Civil Defense Drill" (1955)

Rustin helped lead a 1955 protest by the War Resisters League and FOR against
"Operation Alert," a federally mandated drill in which citizens rehearsed for a possible nuclear attack, and issued this statement explaining his actions.

Even in war time civil liberties are not totally abolished in countries with a
democratic tradition and we do not believe that the government has a right in
effect to create a state of martial law in connection with a peacetime civil de-

fense demonstration. We were, and are, therefore, convinced that on June 15 we were acting within our rights in a conscientious effort to bear our witness and to bring our convictions to the attention of our fellow citizens. We wish to state briefly the nature of these convictions.

Our refusal on grounds of conscience to take part in the mock demonstration on June 15, 1955, and in particular to "take shelter" at the time of the alert, was not based on insensitiveness to human suffering. The organizations to which we belong and their members devote a great deal of attention as a matter of fact to works of mercy and good-will. . . .

The United States government is devoting the major part of its budget and vast resources to preparation, not only for H-bomb, but also for biological and bacteriological war. The kind of public and highly publicized demonstrations held on June 15, are essentially a part of war preparation. They accustom people to the idea of war, to acceptance of war as probably inevitable and as somehow right if waged in "defense" and "retaliation." The fact that President Eisenhower used his talk to the nation at the close of the three-day exercise of the Executive Department in a secret hide-out to promote the Reserve Training Act – i.e., Universal Military Training – was fully in line with the basic purpose of the June 15 demonstration. . . .

We are opposed to all war. We do not believe that any nation has the moral or spiritual right to visit atomic and biological destruction on any other people at any time or for any reason whatever. Those of us who are Christians declare this in the name of Christ; but, on whatever grounds, it is for all of us a profound conscientious conviction. To take part in what we regarded as essentially an exercise in preparation for war was, therefore, impossible for us.

Apart from ultimate moral or spiritual considerations binding upon the individual, we believe that it is politically a disastrous error for the United States to depend for security and for the preservation of democratic values in this age upon nuclear and biological armament. We should instead remove the causes of war, devoting our material, intellectual and spiritual resources to combating poverty and disease throughout the world and supporting the struggles of the underprivileged peoples to end oppression and achieve free and equal status. This would serve to create the environment of justice and good-will in which peace can flourish and mankind live in safety.

*   *   *

"Report on Montgomery, Alabama" (1956)

Rustin analyzed the Montgomery bus boycott and its implications for race relations in the South and North in a report to the War Resisters League.

The Montgomery Boycott:

a. The leadership in general is exploring the principles and tactics of non-violence. All the leaders are clear that they will have no part in starting violence. There is, however, considerable confusion on the question as to whether violence is justified in retaliation to violence directed against the Negro community. At present there is no careful, non-violent preparation for any such extreme situation.

b. The Reverend Martin Luther King, Jr., leader of the Montgomery Improvement Association, which is organizing the non-violent protest, is developing a decidedly Gandhi-like view and recognizes there is a tremendous educational job to be done within the Negro community. He is eagerly learning all that he can about non-violence and evidence indicates that he is emerging as a regional symbol of non-violent resistance in the deep South.

c. Until recently the Montgomery Improvement Association had no constructive program. Now, however, such an educational and work program is underway. Huge prayer meetings and symbols, including slogans, discussions and songs, are designed to keep the movement going. The car pool, substitute transportation for the Negro community, is efficiently operated and utilizes constructively the energies of many scores of the secondary leadership.

d. The leadership, comprising about one hundred Negro men and women, from all classes, is courageous. Many have been arrested and are prepared to go to jail. Their trials began March 19.

e. The Negro community of approximately 45,000 people is almost to the man behind the protest, refuses to use the buses, contributes over $2,000 weekly to help with the car pool and will not return to the buses until their minimal demands are met. The movement is strong because it is religious as well as political. It has been built upon the most stable institution of the southern Negro community – the Church. There is no evidence of Communist infiltration.

f. The protest is a rank and file movement. No particular person or persons began it. It arose from a very general response to the arrest of a respectable Negro woman who refused to move to the rear of a bus. The community resented her treatment; the community began to act. Later the ministers began to give guidance to a movement which they had created.

The Importance of the Montgomery Protest:

a. Through the non-violent action in Montgomery, Negroes, North and South, have come to see that many of the stereotypes they have held about themselves are not necessarily true. The protest has given them a sense of pride and dignity and they now believe,

1. that they can "stick together"
2. that their leaders do not necessarily "sell out"
3. that violence, such as the bombing of the leaders' homes, does not necessarily "any longer intimidate"
4. that their church and ministers "are now militant" . . . 25 of those arrested are ministers
5. that they have found a new direct-action method that is bound "to spread over the deep South"

b. Montgomery has convinced many southern Negroes that certain elements in the white southern community do not intend to see them make any progress. The Negroes see evidence of this in the fact that their prerequisites for returning to the buses are merely conditions prevailing in other southern cities already. The protest leaders seek

1. courteous treatment on the buses
2. first-come-first-served seating *within the segregation pattern* while the courts determine the legality of intra-state segregation
3. *some* Negro drivers on buses serving predominantly Negro areas.

Why, the Negroes ask, are white people unwilling to grant these simple requests? The answer, they believe, is that a line has now been drawn against any final abolition of segregation. This has led the Negro in Montgomery to redouble his effort since his treatment on the buses is a long-standing grievance and has caused Negroes in other areas of the South to believe all is lost unless they vigorously struggle for justice now. . . .

Two Important Considerations:

a. We in the North should bear in mind that the most important thing we can do to help the Montgomery situation is to press now for total integration in the North. Montgomery is important if it stimulates us to greater action where we are.
b. Montgomery is also significant because it reveals to a world sick with violence that non-violent resistance has relevance today in the United States against forces that are prepared to use extreme measures to crush it. This is a very real educational factor for all people to utilize who are working for world peace.

*   *   *

"The Time is NOW" (1963)

Rustin produced this promotional pamphlet for the March on Washington.

Wednesday, August 28, 1963

America faces a crisis . . .

Millions of citizens are unemployed . . .

Millions are denied freedom . . .

The twin evils of discrimination and economic deprivation plague the nation. They rob all people, Negro and white, of dignity, self-respect and freedom. They impose a special burden upon the Negro who is denied the right to vote, refused access to public accommodations, forced to accept inferior education and relegated to sub-standard ghetto housing.

One hundred years after the Emancipation Proclamation, the American Negro still bears the brunt of economic exploitation, the indignity of second-class citizenship, and ignominy of slave wages.

The rate of Negro unemployment is almost three times higher than that of white workers, breeding misery, frustration and degradation in every community—North and South.

Discrimination in education and in apprenticeship training renders Negroes, Puerto Ricans and other minorities helpless in our mechanized, industrial society. Shunted to relief, to charity, or to living by their wits, the jobless are driven to despair, to crime, to hatred and to violence.

Yet, despite this crisis . . .

Southern Democrats and reactionary Republicans in Congress are still working to defeat any effective civil rights legislation. They fight against the rights of all workers and minority groups. They are the sworn enemies of freedom and justice. They proclaim states rights in order to destroy human rights.

The Southern Democrats came to power by disenfranchising the Negro people. They know that as long as black workers are voteless, exploited, depressed and underpaid the fight of white workers for decent wages and working conditions will fail. They know that semi-slavery for one means semi-slavery for all.

We oppose these forces. We appeal for unity to destroy this century-long hoax.

WE CALL UPON ALL AMERICANS,
REGARDLESS OF RACE OR CREED,
TO JOIN
THE MARCH ON WASHINGTON
for freedom

- To demand that Congress pass a civil rights bill that will restore the constitutional rights now denied the Negro people.
- To assure neither watering down, nor compromise, nor filibuster against civil rights legislation by either political party.
- To offer a great witness to the basic moral principle of human equality and brotherhood. . . .

March on Washington for Jobs and Freedom
170 West 130th Street, New York 27, N.Y.
FI 8-1900
A. Philip Randolph, Director
Bayard Rustin, Deputy Director

* * *

"Statement by Bayard Rustin" (August 14, 1963)

On the eve of the March on Washington, Rustin responded to charges by Senator Strom Thurmond that he had been a draft dodger and a Communist.

I wish to comment on two charges leveled against me by Senator Strom Thurmond.

The first charge is that I was a draft-dodger during World War II. This is demonstrably false. As a Quaker, I refused to participate in World War II on grounds of conscientious objection. I notified my draft board accordingly. When I was sentenced to 28 months, the judge was sufficiently impressed with the sincerity of my pacifist convictions to allow me three weeks, without bail, to complete my work for the Congress of Racial Equality (CORE) before serving my sentence.

My activities in the pacifist and Quaker organizations are well known. My adherence to nonviolence in the civil rights movement is an outgrowth of the philosophical pacifism I came to accept in the course of those activities. One may quarrel with the conscientious objector, but it is neither fair nor accurate to call him a draft-dodger. I did not dodge the draft. I openly and vigorously opposed it. Twenty eight months imprisonment was the price I willingly paid for my convictions.

Senator Thurmond charges me with Communism. I am not now and never have been a member of the Communist Party. More than twenty years ago, while a student at the City College of New York, I was a member of the Young Communist League. In 1938 when I joined the YCL, I thought it was genuinely interested in peace and in racial justice. Those were the years of the Hitler-Stalin pact, when pacifists could feel relatively comfortable in the YCL. In 1941 when Hitler attacked the Soviet Union, the YCL line changed overnight. The fight for peace and for civil rights was declared subordinate to the defense of the Soviet Union. The League instructed me to stop agitating for integration of the Armed Forces on the grounds that this impaired the war effort.

I have never been willing to subordinate the just demands of my people to the foreign or domestic policy of any nation. I did not then, and I do not now, consider acquiescence in injustice the road to any kind of true democracy. Accordingly, I left the YCL in 1941.

Even before that year, my Quaker beliefs had conflicted with the basic aims and practices of the YCL. Those beliefs, strengthened over the years, remain incompatible with Communism. . . .

I am not the first of my race to have been falsely attacked by spokesmen of the Confederacy. But even from them a minimal affection for the facts should be expected. Senator Thurmond's remarks were a disgrace to the United States Senate and a measure of the desperation of the segregationist cause.

With regard to Senator Thurmond's attack on my morality, I have no comment. By religious training and fundamental philosophy, I am disinclined to put myself in the position of having to defend my own moral character. Questions in this area should properly be directed to those who have entrusted me with my present responsibilities.

*   *   *

Pledge by March on Washington Participants (August 28, 1963)

Text of pledge read by Rustin at conclusion of March on Washington and agreed to by the audience, promising to continue to work for its goals.

PLEDGE

Standing before the Lincoln Memorial on the 28th of August, in the Centennial Year of Emancipation, I affirm my complete personal commitment to the struggle for Jobs and Freedom for all Americans.

To fulfill that commitment, I pledge that I will not relax until victory is won.

I pledge that I will join and support all actions undertaken in good faith in accord with the time-honored democratic tradition of non-violent protest, of peaceful assembly and petition, and of redress through the courts and the legislative process.

I pledge to carry the message of the March to my friends and neighbors back home and to arouse them to an equal commitment and an equal effort. I will march and I will write letters. I will demonstrate and I will vote. I will work to make sure that my voice and those of my brothers ring clear and determined from every corner of our land.

I pledge my heart and my mind and my body, unequivocally and without regard to personal sacrifice, to the achievement of social peace through social justice.

*　　*　　*

"From Protest to Politics: The Future of the Civil Rights Movement" (February 1965)

Rustin's classic expression of the need for coalition politics to replace demonstrations as the primary strategy of the American civil rights movement, published in Commentary magazine.

I.

The decade spanned by the 1954 Supreme Court decision on school desegregation and the Civil Rights Act of 1964 will undoubtedly be recorded as the period in which the legal foundations of racism in America were destroyed. To be sure, pockets of resistance remain; but it would be hard to quarrel with the assertion that the elaborate legal structure of segregation and discrimination, particularly in relation to public accommodations, has virtually collapsed. On the other hand, without making light of the human sacrifices involved in the direct-action tactics (sit-ins, freedom rides, and the rest) that were so instrumental to this achievement, we must recognize that in desegregating public accommodations, we affected institutions which are relatively peripheral both to the American socio-economic order and to the fundamental conditions of life of the Negro people. In a highly industrialized, 20th-century civilization, we hit Jim Crow precisely where it was most anachronistic, dispensable, and vulnerable—in hotels, lunch counters, terminals, libraries, swimming pools, and the like. For in these forms, Jim Crow does impede the flow of commerce in the broadest sense: it is a nuisance in a society on the move (and on the make). Not surprisingly therefore, it was the most mobility-conscious and relatively liberated groups in the Negro community—lower-middle-class college students—who launched the attack that brought down this imposing but hollow structure.

The term "classical" appears especially apt for this phase of the civil rights movement. But in the few years that have passed since the first flush of sit-ins, several developments have taken place that have complicated matters enormously.

One is the shifting focus of the movement in the South, symbolized by Birmingham; another is the spread of the revolution to the North; and the third, common to the other two, is the expansion of the movement's base in the Negro community. To attempt to disentangle these three strands is to do violence to reality. David Danzig's perceptive article, "The Meaning of Negro Strategy," correctly saw in the Birmingham events the victory of the concept of collective struggle over individual achievement as the road to Negro freedom. And Birmingham remains the unmatched symbol of grass-roots protest involving all strata of the black community. It was also in this most industrialized of Southern cities that the single-issue demands of the movement's classical stage gave way to the "package deal." No longer were Negroes satisfied with integrating lunch counters. They now sought advances in employment, housing, school integration, police protection, and so forth.

Thus, the movement in the South began to attack areas of discrimination which were not so remote from the Northern experience as were Jim Crow lunch counters. At the same time, the interrelationship of these apparently distinct areas became increasingly evident. What is the value of winning access to public accommodations for those who lack money to use them? The minute the movement faced this question, it was compelled to expand its vision beyond race relations to economic relations, including the role of education in modern society. And what also became clear is that all these interrelated problems, by their very nature, are not soluble by private, voluntary efforts but require government action – or politics. . . . A conscious bid for *political power* is being made, and in the course of that effort a tactical shift is being effected: direct-action techniques are being subordinated to a strategy calling for the building of community institutions or power bases. Clearly, the implications of this shift reach far beyond Mississippi. What began as a protest movement is being challenged to translate itself into a political movement. Is this the right course? And if it is, can the transformation be accomplished?

II.

The very decade which has witnessed the decline of legal Jim Crow has also seen the rise of *de facto* segregation in our most fundamental socio-economic institutions. More Negroes are unemployed today than in 1954, and the unemployment gap between the races is wider. The median income of Negroes has dropped from 57 per cent to 54 per cent of that of whites. A higher percentage of Negro workers is now concentrated in jobs vulnerable to automation than was the case ten years ago. More Negroes attend *de facto* segregated schools today than when the Supreme Court handed down its famous decision; while school integration proceeds at a snail's pace in the South, the number of Northern schools with an excessive proportion of minority youth proliferates. And behind this is the continuing growth of racial slums, spreading over our central cities and trapping Negro youth is a milieu which, whatever its legal definition, sows an unimaginable demoralization. Again, legal niceties aside, a resident of a racial ghetto lives in segregated housing, and more Negroes fall into this category than ever before. . . .

III.

Let me sum up what I have thus far been trying to say: The civil rights movement is evolving from a protest movement into a full-fledged *social movement* – an evolution calling its very name into question. It is now concerned not merely with removing the barriers to full *opportunity* but with achieving the fact of *equality*. From sit-ins and freedom rides we have gone into rent strikes, boycotts, community organization, and political action. As a consequence of this natural evolution, the Negro today finds himself stymied by obstacles of far greater magnitude than the legal barriers he was attacking before: automation, urban decay, *de facto* school segregation. These are problems which, while conditioned by Jim Crow, do not vanish upon its demise. They are more deeply rooted in our socio-economic order; they are the result of the total society's failure to meet not only the Negro's needs, but human needs generally. . . .

How are these radical objectives to be achieved? The answer is simple, deceptively so: *through political power.*

There is a strong moralistic strain in the civil rights movement which would remind us that power corrupts, forgetting that the absence of power also corrupts. But this is not the view I want to debate here, for it is waning. Our problem is posed by those who accept the need for political power but do not understand the nature of the object and therefore lack sound strategies for achieving it; they tend to confuse political institutions with lunch counters.

A handful of Negroes, acting alone, could integrate a lunch counter by strategically locating their bodies so as *directly* to interrupt the operation of the proprietor's will; their numbers were relatively unimportant. In politics, however, such a confrontation is difficult because the interests involved are merely *represented*. In the execution of a political decision a direct confrontation may ensue. . . . But in arriving at a political decision, numbers and organizations are crucial, especially for the economically disenfranchised. . . .

Neither the Civil Rights Movement nor the country's twenty million black people can win political power alone. We need allies. The future of the Negro struggle depends on whether the contradictions of this society can be resolved by a coalition of progressive forces which becomes the *effective* political majority in the Untied States. I speak of the coalition which staged the March on

Washington, passed the Civil Rights Act, and laid the basis for the Johnson landslide – Negroes, trade unionists, liberals, and religious groups.

There are those who argue that a coalition strategy would force the Negro to surrender his political independence to white liberals, that he would be neutralized, deprived of his cutting edge, absorbed into the Establishment. Some who take this position urged last year that votes be withheld from the Johnson-Humphrey ticket as a demonstration of the Negro's political power. Curiously enough, these people who sought to demonstrate power through the non-exercise of it, also point to the Negro "swing vote" in crucial urban areas as the source of the Negro's independent political power. But here they are closer to being right: the urban Negro vote will grow in importance in the coming years. If there is anything positive in the spread of the ghetto, it is the potential political power base thus created and to realize this potential is one of the most challenging and urgent tasks before the civil rights movement. If the movement can wrest leadership of the ghetto vote from the machines, it will have acquired an organized constituency such as other major groups in our society now have.

But we must also remember that the effectiveness of a swing vote depends solely on "other" votes. It derives its power from them. In that sense, it can never be "independent," but must opt for one candidate or the other, even if by default. Thus coalitions are inescapable, however tentative they may be. And this is the case in all but those few situations in which Negroes running on an independent ticket might conceivable win. "Independence," in other words, is not a value in itself. The issue is which coalition to join and how to make it responsive to your program. Necessarily there will be compromise. But the difference between expediency and morality in politics is the difference between selling out a principle and making smaller concessions to win larger ones. The leader who shrinks from this task reveals not his purity but his lack of political sense.

The task of molding a political movement out of the March on Washington coalition is not simple, but no alternatives have been advanced. We need to choose our allies on the basis of common political objectives. It has become fashionable in some no-win Negro circles to decry for the white liberal as the main enemy (his hypocrisy is what sustains racism); by virtue of this reverse recitation of the reactionary's litany (liberalism leads to socialism which leads to Communism) the Negro is left in majestic isolation, except for a tiny band of fervent white initiates. But the objective fact is that *Eastland and Goldwater* are the main enemies – they and the opponents of civil rights, of the war on poverty, of medicare, of social security, of federal aid to education, of unions, and so forth. The labor movement, despite its obvious faults, has been the largest single organized force in this country pushing for progressive social legislation. And where the Negro-labor-liberal axis is weak, as in the farm belt, it was the religious groups that were most influential in rallying support for the Civil Rights Bill.

The durability of the coalition was interestingly tested during the election. I do not believe that the Johnson landslide proved the "white backlash" to be a myth. It proved, rather, that economic interests are more fundamental than prejudice: the backlashers decided that loss of social security was, after all, too high a price to pay for a slap at the Negro. This lesson was a valuable first step in re-educating such people, and it must be kept alive, for the civil rights movement will be advanced only to the degree that social and economic welfare gets to be inextricably entangled with civil rights.

The 1964 elections marked a turning point in American politics. The Democratic landslide was not merely the result of a negative reaction to Goldwaterism; it was also the expression of a majority liberal consensus. The near unanimity with which Negro votes joined in that expression was, I am convinced, a vindication of the July 25th statement by Negro leaders calling for a strategic turn toward political action and a temporary curtailment of mass demonstrations. . . .

It may be premature to predict a Southern Democratic party of Negroes and white moderates and a Republican Party of refugee racists and economic conservatives, but there certainly is a strong tendency toward such a realignment; and an additional 3.6 million Negroes of voting age in the eleven Southern states are still to be heard from. Even the *tendency* toward disintegration of the Democratic party's racist wing defines a new context for Presidential and liberal strategy in the congressional battles ahead. Thus the Negro vote (North as well as South), while not *decisive* in the Presidential race, was enormously effective. It was a dramatic element of a historic mandate which contains vast possibilities and dangers that will fundamentally affect the future course of the civil rights movement. . . .

None of this *guarantees* vigorous executive or legislative action. . . . Goldwater's capture of the Republican party forced into the Democratic camp many disparate elements which do not belong there, Big Business being the major example. Johnson, who wants to be President "of all people," may try to keep his new coalition together by sticking close to the political center. But if he decides to do this, it is unlikely that even his political genius will be able to hold together a coalition so inherently unstable and rife with contradictions. It must come apart. Should it do so while Johnson is pursuing a centrist course, then the mandate will have been wastefully dissipated. However, if the mandate is seized upon to set fundamental changes in motion, then the basis can be laid for a new mandate, a new coalition including hitherto inert and dispossessed strata of the population.

Here is where the cutting edge of the civil rights movement can be applied. We must see to it that the reorganization of the "consensus party" proceeds along lines which will make it an effective vehicle for social reconstruction, a role it cannot play so long as it furnishes Southern racism with its national political power. (One of Barry Goldwater's few attractive ideas was that the Dixiecrats belong with him in the same party.) And nowhere has the civil rights movement's political cutting edge been more magnificently demonstrated than at Atlantic City, where the Mississippi Freedom Democratic Party not only secured recognition as a bona fide component of the national party, but in the process routed the representatives of the most rabid racists – the white Mississippi and Alabama delegations. While I still believe that the MFDP made a tactical error in spurning the compromise, there is no question that they launched a political revolution whose logic is the displacement of Dixiecrat power. They launched that revolution within a major political institution and as part of a coalitional effort.

The role of the civil rights movement in the reorganization of American political life is programmatic as well as strategic. We are challenged now to broaden our social vision, to develop functional programs with concrete objectives. We need to propose alternatives to technological unemployment, urban decay, and the rest. We need to be calling for public works and training, for national economic planning, for federal aid to education, for attractive public housing – all this on a sufficiently massive scale to make a difference. We need to protest the notion that our integration into American life, so long delayed, must now proceed in an atmosphere of competitive scarcity instead of in the security of abundance which technology makes possible. We cannot claim to have answers to all the complex problems of modern society. That is too much to ask of a movement still battling barbarism in Mississippi. But we can agitate the right questions by probing at the contradictions which still stand in the way of the "Great Society." The questions having been asked, motion must begin in the larger society, for there is a limit to what Negroes can do alone.

*   *   *

Open Letter, Staughton Lynd to Bayard Rustin, April 19, 1965

Antiwar activist Staughton Lynd wrote this letter to Rustin in 1965, accusing him of "red-baiting" the New Left and abandoning it on the Vietnam issue.

Dear Bayard:

I was distressed that you took part in Red-baiting the March on Washington against the war in Vietnam. I want to know why.

I refer to the statement you issued along with Norman Thomas, Robert Gilmore and others, which said in part: "we welcome the cooperation of all those groups and individuals who, like ourselves, believe in the need for an independent peace movement, not committed to any form of totalitarianism or drawing inspiration from the foreign policy of any government."

I assume your implication was not that Students for a Democratic Society, described by the New York Times as "non-Communist," is committed to totalitarianism or inspired from abroad. . . . SNCC participated in the march wholeheartedly. But you and your associates made this your reason for not joining the march; indeed I am told that you personally did your best to prevent the march.

What I think this means is that you do not believe in a independent peace movement. You believe in a peace movement dependent on the Johnson Administration. The New York Post said of your statement that it hoped the marchers will "get the meaning of this message," that meaning being:

> Americans may reasonably differ with some aspects of the President's course. But, especially in the aftermath of Mr. Johnson's call for "unconditional" negotiations, there is no justification for transforming the march into a frenzied, one-sided anti-American show.

In other words, we can oppose this horrible war only as house radicals, only as court jesters. And you, who should be leading us in civil disobedience, have gone along.

Why, Bayard? You must know in your heart that your position betrays the essential moralism which you have taught myself and others over the years.

The lesson of your apostasy on Vietnam appears to be that the gains for American Negroes you advise them to seek through coalition politics within the Democratic Party come only at a price. The price is to become a "national civil rights leader" who delivers his constituency. The price is to urge "jobs and freedom" for Americans only. The price, at a time when we desperately need to stand together and transcend old bitternesses, is to set the stage for a government witch-hunt. The price is to make our brothers in Vietnam a burnt offering on the altar of political expediency.

I appeal to you: are you sure what you are doing is what you want to do?

Staughton Lynd

*   *   *

"A Freedom Budget For All Americans" (1967)

Rustin's promotional pamphlet for his Freedom Budget, which proposed that the federal government guarantee every American comprehensive social services.

The Freedom Budget is a practical, step-by-step plan for wiping out poverty in America during the next 10 years.

It will mean more money in your pocket. It will mean better schools for your children. It will mean better homes for you and your neighbors. It will mean clean air to breathe and comfortable cities to live in. It will mean adequate medical care when you are sick.

So where does the "Freedom" come in?

For the first time, everyone in America who is fit and able to work will have a job. For the first time, everyone who can't work, or shouldn't be working, will have an income adequate to live in comfort and dignity. And that is freedom. For freedom from want is the basic freedom from which all others flow.

This nation has learned that it must provide freedom for all if any of us is to be free. We have learned that half-measures are not enough. We know that continued unfair treatment of part of our people breeds misery and waste that are both morally indefensible and a threat to all who are better off.

As A. Philip Randolph put it: "Here in these United States, where there can be no economic or technical excuse for it, poverty is not only a private tragedy but, in a sense, a public crime. It is above all a challenge to our morality."

The Freedom Budget would make that challenge the lever we can grasp to wipe out poverty in a decade.

Pie in the sky?

Not on your life. Just simple recognition of the fact that we, as a nation, never had it so good. That we have the ability and the means to provide adequately for everyone. That simple justice requires us to see that everyone – white or black; in the city or on the farm; fisherman or mountaineer – may have his share in our national wealth. . . .

The Freedom Budget provides seven basic objectives, which taken together will achieve this great goal within 10 years. They are:

1. To provide *full employment* for all who are willing and able to work, including those who need education or training to make them willing and able.
2. To assure *decent and adequate wages* to all who work.
3. To assure a *decent living standard* to those who cannot or should not work.
4. To *wipe out slum ghettos* and provide decent homes for all Americans.
5. To provide *decent medical care and adequate educational opportunities* to all Americans, at a cost they can afford.
6. To *purify our air and water* and develop our transportation and natural resources on a scale suitable to our growing needs.
7. To unite sustained full employment with sustained *full production and high economic growth*.

The Freedom Budget shows how to do all this without a raise in taxes and without a single make-work job – by planning prudently NOW to use the economic growth of the future, and with adequate attention to our international commitments.

The key is jobs.

We can all recognize that the major cause of poverty could be eliminated, if enough decently paying jobs were available for everyone willing and able to work. And we can also recognize that with enough jobs for all, a basic cause of discrimination among job-seekers would automatically disappear.

What we must also recognize is that we now have the means of achieving complete employment – at no increased cost, with no radical change in our economic system, and at no cost to our present national goals – if we are willing to commit ourselves totally to this achievement.

No doles. No skimping on national defense. No tampering with private supply and demand.

Just an enlightened self-interest, using what we have in the best possible way.

By giving the poor a chance to become dignified wage earners, we will be generating the money to finance the improvements we all need – rich and poor alike. And we would be doing it by making new jobs with new money, so that no one who is now earning his own living would suffer.

The Freedom Budget recognizes that the Federal government must take the lead in attaining the eradication of poverty.

The Federal government alone represents all 200 million American individuals. It alone has the resources for a comprehensive job. And it has the responsibility for fulfilling the needs which are the basis for the Freedom Budget plan. . . .

Where will the money come from?

The Freedom Budget recognizes that we cannot spend what we do not produce. It also recognizes that we must spend wisely what we do produce.

It proposes that a portion of our future growth – one thirteenth of what can reasonably be expected to be available – be earmarked for the eradication of poverty. The Freedom Budget proposed outlay of $185 billion in 10 years sounds like a great deal of money, and it is a great deal of money.

But it will come from the expansion of our economy that will in part be the result of wise use of that very $185 billion. It will build homes and schools, provide recreation areas and hospitals. It will train teachers and nurses.

It will provide adequate incomes to millions who now do not have them. And those millions will in turn buy goods they cannot now buy.

So the wage earner of today will benefit as well. His earnings will go up and his enjoyment of life will be increased. The opportunities for private enterprise will increase.

The breeding grounds of crime and discontent will be diminished in the same way that draining a swamp cuts down the breeding of mosquitoes, and the causes of discrimination will be considerably reduced. . . .

The Freedom Budget, then, is a new call to arms for a final assault on injustice. It is a rallying cry we cannot fail to heed. . . .

For national defense, space technology and all international outlays, the federal budget in 1967 was $64.6 billion. The "Freedom Budget" assumes this figure would rise to $87.5 billion in 1975.

In making this estimate, the Freedom Budget neither endorses nor condemns present military spending policies. It relies on the judgment of informed experts. Obviously, if the international situation improves and a reduction in military spending is in order, so much more money will be available for social needs. But even if military spending increases faster than now envisioned, the Freedom Budget proves that we can afford to carry out the necessary programs. But the abolition of poverty is too precious a goal to be made *contingent* on such a reduction.

*   *   *

Convocation Address, Clark College, March 5, 1968

In this 1968 address to students at historically black Clark College, Rustin explained his beliefs in coalition politics, interracialism, and economic democracy.

. . .Young Negroes are now so frustrated that they are substituting sloganism for analysis. They are examining their navels when they should be examining economic and social programs. They are more concerned with the way they wear their hair and whether or not they are called "black" or "Afro-American" than with developing strategies to solve the problems of housing, poverty, and jobs. No people have ever rid themselves of a difficult social and economic problem by merely examining their own innards or by insisting on a certain name. We do not even understand the nature of the revolution through which we are passing. Here is a stark and befuddling fact: if, tomorrow, every Negro in this country between 17 and 25 became white overnight, every economic problem he now faces would remain. For the problems we face today arise out of basic social and economic contradictions in American society, over and above color. In Appalachia and other areas there are millions of white youngsters who will never have the opportunity to go to college, and who are suffering the same economic hardships that Negroes suffer.

To understand the nature of the problem we are now facing, we have to go back to the 1955-1965 period. That was a period of protest, and protest worked then for one simple reason: we were dealing then with things that protest could affect – public accommodations and the right to vote. All we needed then were a few people who were willing to sit down until something happened. If we sat in restaurants, then sooner or later they were either closed down or integrated.

If we continued to press at the polls, then sooner or later we were permitted to vote. But now we are up against problems which are totally different from public accommodations and voting. We are now asking for decent education, jobs, housing, health and transportation.

Not a single Negro or a single white person had to pay a penny (except for police protection) to integrate public accommodations and to win the right to vote. Now, if we are to get decent housing, schools and jobs, the nation must spend billions and billions of dollars. That is the crucial difference. Thus, many people who marched on Washington in 1963 for Negro dignity are not now prepared to have their taxes raised to make economic dignity truly possible. . . .

In the present period, if we are to have a movement it will come about because we are dealing with the tedious day-to-day task of planning. Brutality alone will not congeal us again.

If our job is to get housing, schools, jobs and better medical care, then there is only one way to get them – and it is not by protest. Protest is not going to pressure Congress into doing those things. We can protest but we can't make that the emphasis. The emphasis must be politics, because if we want billions of dollars from Congress then we've got to create the kind of Congress which is prepared to vote that money. . . .

We must now make a decision. The notion now emerging among young Negro college students that we must have an all-black unity, is as profoundly wrong as any remark I've heard. You can never get people, on the basis of color alone, to unite. . . . You do not organize, never can organize, around blackness alone, or any color alone. You organize around program and philosophy. . . .

Take this . . . slogan, that we want "all-black schools, all black principals, all black teachers." Obviously, we need more Negro principals and more Negro teachers in the school system. But in Harlem there's a school where the parents are saying "we want to make the curriculum, we want to select the principal, and he must be black; we want black supervisors." Now what they don't understand is that out in Queens, there is a white racist woman who says that if they get the right to do that in Harlem then she must get the right to do it in Queens. Therefore, Queens will end up having a fascist school system, and she's going to insist on all-white Protestant principals, all-white Protestant supervisors, and there won't be a Negro admitted anywhere. . . .

We had a March on Washington which made everybody happy. We got the 1964 Civil Rights Bill, and got the 1965 Voting Rights Bill, and we thought everything was going to be alright. Instead, there is now more despair than ever before. There are more Negro children in segregated schools than before the Supreme Court decision. Unemployment among Negro girls is three times the rate among whites of the same age. And the unemployment rate in our major cities for Negro youngsters between 18 and 25 is 40%. The ghettoes are bigger.

Unemployment is higher. Schools are worse. Once again, the great hopes stirred by the protest revolution have been dashed and despair and sloganism have re-emerged.

That is the meaning of the negative aspects of "Black Powerism" today. It is a visceral reaction turned in. People do not believe they can do anything or make any changes in society.

There's only one answer to the problem in the United States, because the country is never going to do anything special for the Negro people. The answer is to join into political alliances to achieve all the programs that will solve poverty for all Americans. . . .

One final point. The Negro will gain nothing economically in this nation simply because he is a Negro. One tenth of the population cannot go to Congress for the billions of dollars which are needed. We must go with other like-minded people: the labor movement, Catholics, Protestants, Jews, liberals and students. Together we must create a political force and a political alliance, or an atmosphere which makes that alliance possible.

Anybody can say to white people, "roll over, we don't need you." But that is not a political expression. The political expression is: We need a coalition of Republican and Democrat white men in the Senate to shut off filibustering so that we can get a housing bill or any other bill. Finally, the alternative to registering and voting, and bringing about a new atmosphere in Washington, the alternative to that is to cop-out and talk about hair, about what name you want to be called, and about soul food. Wearing my hair Afro style, calling myself an Afro-American, and eating all the chitterlings I can find are not going to affect Congress.

What matters is whether I encourage other Negroes to go to the polls and to vote. It is whether I have a political answer to a political problem.

*   *   *

"An Appeal to the Community from Black Trade Unionists" (September 19, 1968)

During the 1968 Ocean Hill-Brownsville school strikes, Rustin authored this advertisement, signed by a group of African-American union officials and printed in New York City's major newspapers, in support of the United Federation of Teachers. By the end of the strikes, most of the officials had disavowed the advertisement and turned against Rustin.

The New York public schools are being struck by the United Federation of Teachers. The atmosphere of the city is charged with tension. Threats have been made, and there is fear of an escalation of violence.

One of the most dangerous aspects of the conflict involving the UFT, the Board of Education, and the Ocean Hill-Brownsville governing board is that it has been portrayed as a racial issue – the UFT versus the black community, the UFT versus decentralization.

Nothing could be more tragic than this distortion. Nothing could more sharply aggravate racial strife or more cruelly prolong the school shut-down.

While we have not always agreed with the UFT, we must now speak out to correct distortions and to set the record straight regarding the current conflict. . . .

Due process is the central issue. It is the right of every worker not to be transferred or fired at the whim of his employer. It is the right of every worker to be judged on his merits – not his color or creed. It is the right of every worker to job security.

These are the rights that black workers have struggled and sacrificed to win for generations. They are not abstractions. They are the black workers' safeguards against being "the last hired and the first fired." We have a long way to go to make these rights a reality. But if they are weakened or disparaged – for whatever reason – in the society at large, we will ultimately be the worst victims.

These rights have been denied to teachers in the Ocean Hill-Brownsville district by the local governing board. The ten teachers dismissed by the board have been found innocent of any wrong-doing by the distinguished black Judge Francis Rivers. Still the local board has refused to reinstate the teachers. This injustice must not be camouflaged by appeals to racial solidarity.

If due process is not won in Ocean Hill-Brownsville, what will prevent white community groups in Queens from firing black teachers – or white teachers with liberal views? . . .

In this context we must ask: Will decentralization lead to apartheid education or to maximum feasible integration? Will teacher unionism – the most powerful force for quality education – be respected or destroyed? Will New York City attract the best teachers available, or will fear and insecurity drive the best teachers out of our school system? . . .

These are the real issues – and they are not racial. The overwhelming majority of black teachers are supporting the UFT strike. They will not be scared off by a small group that substitutes raucous voices for sober thought. And they will not be a party to any campaign to break the Union.

We believe that these teachers deserve the support of the entire community. We owe it to black children to speak out, and not to be silenced or cowed by self-appointed "community representatives" whose influence rests on the threat of intimidation or violence. If we do not make ourselves heard, they will appear to speak for the total black community.

Let us speak bluntly. For the black community, more is at stake than the schools. The issue is also whether the community can run its affairs democratically, with freedom of expression for all points of view, or whether we will be strong-armed by small cliques.

We call upon all New Yorkers to support the principle of due process for which the United Federation of Teachers is struggling. We especially urge the authentic voices of the black community – parents, ministers, and civic leaders – to join us in demanding a fair and just settlement of the teachers' strike.

We appeal to all our black brothers and sisters not to permit their justified frustrations to lead them into strategies and tactics that are self-defeating.

We urge community groups, parent associations and the UFT to build, despite their differences, a working alliance. Only such a combined force is strong enough to combat reaction and powerful enough to create a school system that will truly educate all the children, black and white, of New York City.

*   *   *

Letter, Thelma Griffith to Bayard Rustin, September 20, 1968

Letter from an African-American critical of Rustin's alliance with the United Federation of Teachers during the Ocean Hill-Brownsville dispute.

September 20, 1968

Dear Mr. Rustin,

Your activities in support of Albert Shanker's fight against the Ocean Hill-Brownsville board and minority children in this city, deeply wounds many of us who for years admired and respected you for the leadership you have given to many unpopular causes.

I choose to rationalize your role in this instance, and the influence you brought to bear upon respected black trade unionists, as one come to because you did not stop to adequately investigate the issues, but moved from a deep and emotional loyalty and identification with the trade union movement of America.

Your ad (in support of the United Federation of Teachers) is quite wrong, the issue is not job security for teachers. . . . The issue – the real one – is whether America will remain caught up in its racism to the degree that it will continue to set two sets of standards – one for white and establishment and another for poor and black.

In the face of that kind of dual thinking it behooved you to remember that you were black even before you were male or American, and you were all of these before you were a trade unionist. What warrior in the cause of justice can black children look to, when their males are so turned around that they confuse basic principles with self aggrandizement?

Very truly yours,

Thelma Olivia Griffith

*   *   *

"Black Studies and Inequality" (1969)

In this 1969 article, Rustin decried Black Studies as a "cheap separatist solution" that failed to address the problem of inequality in American social and economic life.

By BAYARD RUSTIN

We're living in a time when everybody is proposing what will make him feel good instead of what will solve the problem at hand. Too many Americans to-day are looking for cheap ways to buy racial peace without paying the price for racial and economic justice. Their response to disorder runs the gamut from white breast beating and masochism and attempts to buy off black separatists or other unrepresentative sections of the Negro community, to growing demands for repression. But social peace and reconciliation between the races can only be purchased at a great price economically, politically and psychologically. . . .

I find great irony in [black students'] demands for separate black studies de-partments, for in essence these students are seeking to impose upon themselves the very conditions of separatism and inequality against which black Americans have struggled since the era of Reconstruction.

To give these students separate courses of study such as soul music and soul lit-erature—things that they can just play with and pass—is no answer to the funda-mental difficulty which is to resolve the conflict between their aspiration—which is a function of their talent and potential—and their ability—the development of which until now has been stunted by segregation. But to accomplish this revolu-tion will require the expenditure of hundreds of thousands of dollars for a larger teaching staff and for remedial efforts, that will improve their performance in mathematics, reading and writing—skills that are useful in the real world.

And if these expensive changes are not made, the cheap separatist solutions will ultimately boomerang. Black studies can provide psychic comfort for the Negro student only temporarily. When they realize that college administrators are playing them cheap—when they realize that New Leftist students and fac-ulty members are using black students for their own revolution by proxy—and when they realize that they are not being given an education but only a paper degree that will hardly improve their economic power in American society, then they will rebel with far greater violence and bitterness than anything we have yet seen. Like black capitalism this is another comfortable and inexpensive "solution" which avoids the profoundly democratic and revolutionary challenge of providing higher education for millions of economically deprived youth both black and white.

I want to make two final points. First, I am opposed to the concept of black studies to the degree that it separates the contribution of black men from the study of American history and society. Racist textbooks and historians have played this game too long for black people to add to the damage that has already been done. The magnificent contribution of black people to America must be recognized and recorded, not only by black people, but also by whites who can benefit at least as much from such knowledge.

And second, we must understand that a multiple society cannot exist where one element in that society, out of its own sense of guilt and masochism, permits any other element to hold a gun at its head in the name of justice. The logic of escalation is inherent in this situation, for soon whites will use the same tactics against blacks, and eventually the triggers will be pulled. It is a destructive thing to all involved.

*   *   *

Letter, Jim Peck to Bayard Rustin, July 22, 1970

This 1970 letter from a former pacifist movement colleague accused Rustin of having become the "housenigger of the Democratic Party." The letter was typical of New Left attacks on Rustin as a turncoat and hypocrite.

July 22, 1970

Dear Bayard,

. . . I feel this is an opportune juncture to express my thoughts on what I view as the *tragedy* of Bayard Rustin. . . . I demonstrated with you, was jailed with you, for 9 years traveled with you . . . and was on that very first 1947 freedom ride with you. . . .

To me it is a tragedy that you have in effect become the housenigger of the Democratic Party (not to mention Meany and Shanker). . . .

Furthermore, *you* didn't have to seek "success" by shifting over to The Establishment. You could have attained *genuine* success by becoming the leader of the peace and/or the black freedom movements. The death of A.J. and Martin left a vacuum of leadership in both movements which is yet to be filled. As I see it, you were the only individual on the scene of calibre to fill it. A.J., in a conversation with me not long before his death, expressed dismay at your withdrawal in 1964 from the peace movement. He would have been doubly dismayed had he lived to witness your role at the Chicago Democratic Convention, your stance on Ocean Hill, the luncheon honoring Humphrey and now the full page ad calling for "providing Israel with the full number of jet aircraft it has requested."

At [our] last get together . . . , I approached you and said: "I have *one* question to ask: how do you live with yourself?" You laughed and responded: "Very well!" "Very well!" I can't help wondering: "how well?" because you used to be a person of conscience. In conclusion I ask—even though my request may be futile—that you consider coming back over to our side. It may not be too late.

Very sincerely,

Jim Peck

*　　*　　*

Statement of Bayard Rustin on Soviet Jewry (1971)

In this 1971 statement, Rustin linked the freedom struggles of Soviet Jews and African Americans.

When I am asked why I, as a black American, speak out against the oppression of Soviet Jewry, my reply is that as a black person, how can I not speak out; how can I not be sensitive to the oppression of a national minority.

What was slavery in the United States if not a form of cultural genocide in which our history, our language, our identity were brutally stamped out? We can understand the meaning of spiritual death that accompanies such oppression, and we can appreciate the overwhelming power of the rebirth of the spirit that is part of the struggle against oppression. Black Americans, therefore, ought to be the first to be concerned with the effort of the Soviet Union to destroy the identity of the Soviet Jews and to crush their struggle for freedom.

Just as white abolitionists fought for the liberation of black slaves, people in the United States, Jewish and non-Jewish, white and black, must fight for the liberation of the Jews in the Soviet Union. The issue is not black or white, poor or gentile, but man's responsibility to fight injustice. Our efforts on behalf of Soviet Jewry will not detract from the struggle for racial equality in America: but will make it more compelling by gracing it with a universal dimension.

*　　*　　*

"Affirmative Action in an Economy of Scarcity" (1974)

Rustin prepared this testimony for the United States House of Representatives Special Sub-Committee on Education in 1974. Criticizing racial quotas, he called instead for "fundamental economic transformation" to aid African Americans.

TO THE SPECIAL SUBCOMMITTEE ON EDUCATION
U.S. HOUSE OF REPRESENTATIVES
CONGRESSMAN JAMES G. O'HARA, CHAIRMAN

The controversy over affirmative action and quotas has raised a number of important issues for American society. Its critics assert that affirmative action, as currently administered by government, amounts to nothing less than reverse discrimination by forcing employers to give minority group and female applicants preference over better-qualified white males. Its supporters, on the other hand, see opposition to affirmative action as further proof of the dominant society's resistance to racial advancement. Some deny that affirmative action formulas devised by the government and the courts constitute quotas; others, however, not only acknowledge that quota directives have been issued, but also justify the quota doctrine as a legitimate method for redressing past and present racial inequities.

The A. Philip Randolph Institute believes the affirmative action concept to be a valid and essential contribution to an over-all program designed to ameliorate the current effects of racial bias, and, ultimately, to achieve the long-sought goal of racial equality. We do not believe, however, that affirmative action can or should occupy the pivotal role in a strategy for racial progress. Affirmative action, we are convinced, can only succeed when combined with programs which have as their objective a much more fundamental economic transformation than affirmative action could bring about.

We are, furthermore, unalterably opposed to the imposition of quotas or any other form of ratio hiring. . . . For now, we would only observe that the implementation of a vigorous affirmative action program which has on occasion included—and we must be honest here—the institution of quota formulas has totally failed to bring about any measurable improvement in the economic condition of the black community. What the imposition of quotas, and the resulting furor they have generated, <u>have</u> accomplished is to exacerbate the differences between blacks and other racial and ethnic groups. And to the degree that these tensions and divisions have been provoked, the time when black people are accepted into American social and economic life as full and equal participants has been that much delayed.

The basic issue raised by the quota controversy has less to do with the behavior of the federal bureaucracy, the role of the court system, or even with the persistence of racial discrimination, than it has to do with a much more basic consideration. That is the issue of how the government is to proceed about the task of fully and peacefully integrating all segments of society and, most particularly, how government is to close the sizable gap between the economic status of blacks and whites. . . .

It seems painfully obvious that an affirmative action program cannot achieve its objectives peacefully and democratically if it must function within the context of scarcity. And we are particularly dismayed by the notion that opportunities can be expanded for some groups at a time when the job market is shrinking for all. You simply cannot elevate significant numbers of blacks or women into better-paying, higher-skilled and more satisfying jobs if those jobs don't exist.

Everyone knows racial discrimination still exists. But the high rate of black unemployment and the reversal of hard won economic gains is not the result of discrimination. All indications, in fact, show that racial prejudice, particularly in the area of employment, is decreasing year-by-year. Black economic decline is a function of much broader economic failures; failures which, moreover, have left their mark on all Americans regardless of race. But as long as inequality is treated as the product of racism, instead of economics, it will seriously divert the attention of society from difficult issues which ultimately must be faced. . . .

There are those who argue that, on a short term basis, quota hiring schemes represent an effective and expedient means of resolving a difficult social problem. But we are convinced that the inherent dangers of the quota principle far outweigh any temporary gains they might bring.

One of the most serious dangers of the quota doctrine is that it will perpetuate the stereotypical—and profoundly mistaken—view that blacks lack the ability and the will to make it on their own. Should quotas become institutionalized as government policy, society, as black educator Thomas Sowell has warned, would no doubt conclude that Negroes "must be given something in order to have something."

Quotas would further entrench the tendency of society to respond to the call for equal opportunity with tokenism. Quotas, in fact, are tokenism taken to its logical conclusion. Blacks object to the token because it downgrades the dignity and abilities of the individual, cheapening both his or her accomplishments and the accomplishments of other blacks to follow. The same is true of the quota, only to a greater degree. The black who benefits from the quota suffers the uncertainty of never knowing whether he made it on his merits, or was simply hired to meet a government decree. As for the dominant white society, it would automatically question the abilities of all blacks, including the overwhelming majority who have succeeded because of their intelligence, skills, and self discipline.

We also believe that the widespread application of quotas would unquestionably lead to the weakening of the merit principle. We recognize that what has been referred to as "merit" often works to the unfair exclusion of certain racial or sexual groups. Thus one of the affirmative action program's most signal accomplishments is to force society to reevaluate the standards which determine who is hired, admitted to college, and so on.

But we are determinedly opposed to a broad assault on the concept of qualifications and standards. For where legitimate standards are weakened, or abolished altogether, it is those who are most vulnerable to discrimination or whimsy who will suffer the most severe consequences. It should be kept in mind that blacks have entered many skilled trades and professions in significantly large numbers. Very often they won their position precisely because their qualifications were superior to other applicants. That blacks are underrepresented in a particular profession does not by itself constitute racial discrimination. Very often the inability of large numbers of blacks to qualify for a particular job is a function of poor educational background. It is for this reason that we believe it is essential for government to ex. . . .

Affirmative action efforts should be largely directed to instances of racial discrimination. In place of ratio or quota formulas, those institutions that have been found guilty of practicing discrimination should be given stiff fines; in other instances of recalcitrance, such as have been exhibited by southern police departments, government should consider asking the courts to institute racially-blind lotteries to determine hiring procedures. We also favor the cancellation of government contracts in cases where racial or sexual bias has been proven. . . .

Government should continue to question the standards and qualifications for hiring. But it should keep in mind that standards are most important to those who are the likely victims of discrimination. The reforming of standards should not mean their weakening or abandonment.

Finally, there should be a realization that affirmative action, by itself, can do little to help blacks unless it operates in a positive economic framework. An affirmative action program cannot find jobs for the unemployed or help the underemployed into better jobs if those jobs do not exist. The most important issue is an economy of growth and expansion. Above all, it must be an economy providing a job for all.

*　　*　　*

"Integration Statement" (1978)

Rustin authored this reaffirmation of his belief in interracialism in 1978.

There is a false and tragic notion abroad in America today—that integration is dead. It isn't though there are some people who wish it were. They include the traditional enemies of integration, those who have always wanted an America rigidly segregated by race, religion and ethnic background. Today they have new allies, those members of the very minority groups that have the most to gain from an open society, but who insist nonetheless the destinies of their peoples can best be worked out in isolation. Theirs is the counsel of despair.

We believe there is hope. In the past two decades there has been significant progress toward integration—in education, jobs, politics, housing and the use of public facilities. Insufficient though this progress has been, it is *still* progress. And it is blind folly to disparage or ignore it. Integration remains, therefore, a realistic and feasible objective. It is also, needless to say, of vital importance to the social and moral health of this nation. We are moved to reaffirm our full, unalterable allegiance to the goal of an integrated, democratic, plural society. Integration, as the word is used here, should not be confused with the idea of America as a "melting pot" which has little relevance to our society today. We believe that black Americans and all minority Americans should take pride in their distinct cultures and heritages. We also believe in a "black power" that expresses itself in economic and political advance.

But we denounce a pride that infects its possessors with suspicion and hatred of the members of all other groups. We reject a society of "we" and "they." We also reject an entrepreneurship that believes the economic problems of the ghetto and barrio can be solved in small shops and plants and family enterprises. We reject the romanticizing of the ghetto as a fit place for human habitation.

The racist nature of our institutions makes it inevitable that we shall have segregated schools and segregated communities in this country for some time to come. But for God's sake let us not pretend, as the separatists do, that that's a boon. Let us recognize those walls for what they are—shameful evidence of centuries of injustice; barriers to fulfillment, cages in whose confinement inhabitants become embittered and wild. And let us also recognize that the only thing to do with the ghetto is to do away with it. . . .

We must act at various levels at the same time. The effort to rescue black children from self-hatred, by inculcating a sense of pride in their origins and history, must go on at the same time they are absorbing the basic skills they need to live and thrive in America. Power bases must be built in order to prepare minorities to play meaningful roles in the government of our cities, states and nation. Our housing and job programs must have as one of their principal objectives the creation of integrated communities and integrated work forces.

The very enormity of the task moves us beyond the tiny, private enterprises that so many separatists advocate. Only one entity in our nation has sufficient power to undertake the task we see before us and that is the Federal government. All our energies must be bent to make the Federal government responsive in all its programs to the desperate needs of the poor and the oppressed for in denial of those needs lies the destruction of our present democratic system.

The government we envision can only be achieved through the cooperative effort of all people who want to live and work together. We reject violence with the same unbending conviction that we reject separatism.

Our goal is a restructuring of society by all of us, so that it reflects the immense richness of our variety. We want a society that welcomes our contributions; a society in which we catch glimpses of ourselves in our newspapers, textbooks, movie and TV screens, in all our agencies and councils of government. We want a society that does not press us into molds but lets us break molds and live, so long as we hurt nobody, lives of individual and collective fulfillment.

That is what we mean by an integrated society. And toward the achievement of such a society we now rededicate ourselves.

*   *   *

"Black Americans Urge Admission of the Indochinese Refugees" (1979)

Rustin prepared this newspaper advertisement on behalf of Asian refugees in 1979. As he had with Soviet Jews, Rustin linked the refugees' plight to that of African Americans.

Throughout non-Communist Asia, thousands of unfortunate refugees from Vietnam, Laos and Cambodia languish in make-shift camps. For most, the future offers frightening prospects: social ostracism in countries to which they fled, endless unemployment, and—even worse—deportation to their homelands resulting in almost certain death.

As concerned citizens of the black community—a community which itself continues to endure widespread economic deprivation—we sympathize with our Asian brothers and sisters in the refugee camps. But our concern must transcend the safe boundaries of mere sympathy. We must move toward action.

Many well-meaning Americans have argued that action on this pressing problem is unworkable in economic terms and potentially explosive. We recognize the scandalous state of America's economy—especially its devastating manifestations in the black community—and we realize that any program to assist these refugees will entail modest economic costs. Yet, we oppose the dehumanizing tendency of placing price tags on the head of Indochinese refugees.

In the past, America has displayed an uncanny ability to adapt to unusual and seemingly impossible situations. We believe that America can once again reach out to an embattled minority—these refugees—and offer safe haven and hope.

Thus, we call upon President Carter and the United States Congress to facilitate the entrance of these refugees into the United States in the same spirit that we have urged our country to accept the victims of South Africa's apartheid.

Through our arduous struggle for civil, political and economic rights in America, we have learned a fundamental lesson: the battle against human misery is indivisible. Our continuing struggle for economic and political freedom is inextricably linked to the struggle of Indochinese refugees who also seek freedom. If our government lacks compassion for these dispossessed human beings, it is difficult to believe that the same government can have much compassion for America's black minority, or for America's poor.

*   *   *

Letter, Bayard Rustin to Yale University, September 17, 1984

Rustin wrote to the Yale University administration in support of its striking clerical and technical workers in 1984.

September 17, 1984

Dear _____:

Last May I had the great privilege of receiving an honorary degree from Yale University, and thus became at least partially a member of the Yale community in the same way that you did.

Yale was gracious and generous in honoring me for my work on behalf of civil rights and justice for working people.

Having been honored in that way, I feel an obligation to speak out about the very disturbing labor dispute which embroils Yale, and which has resulted in the calling of a strike by the union representing the clerical and technical employees. The strike is to begin September 26, 1984.

82% of these employees are women, and 13% are black. It is troubling to me to learn that the average full-time salary for these employees (including many with skilled and responsible jobs, and many years of service) is only $13,424. All of us can appreciate that this is not a salary on which one can live decently, and it is disturbing to realize that many in this overwhelmingly female group are the sole or principal support of the their families. . . .

I cannot help but feel that the University which went out of its way to honor me for my life's work is, at the same time, failing, in its dealings with its own workforce, to appreciate the application of the principles for which I have stood.

It is also dismaying that the University cannot find a way to resolve these issues with the employees' Union. I had an opportunity to meet with the rank and file members of the Union, and I found them to be sincere, constructive, and dedicated to a positive, democratic Union which they hope will be accepted as an integral part of the University community. I had the strong impression that they do not seek conflict with Yale, but find themselves this fall with no other honorable alternative.

[I am sending Yale] a statement which urges Yale University's administration to negotiate with all the intensity, fairness, and commitment it can muster to avoid a damaging strike, and to put Yale firmly on record, in practice as well as in theory, as being a leader in the national struggle to end economic discrimination against women and minorities.

Sincerely,

Bayard Rustin

*   *   *

Letter, Bayard Rustin to New York City Councilwoman Priscilla Wooten, March 22, 1985

By the 1980s, Rustin had become an advocate for homosexual rights. In this letter, he urged support for a gay rights bill that was passed by the New York City Council in 1986.

March 22, 1985

Honorable Priscilla Wooten
City Council
City Hall
New York, N.Y. 10007

Dear Councilmember Wooten:

It has been brought to my attention that you have not supported Intro One (also known as the "Gay Rights Bill"). Beyond this I understand that you have failed to vote for a discharge motion to place this matter before the full City Council.

As one who has worked for 50 years to expand the rights of all Americans— women, blacks, Hispanics, Japanese-Americans, the handicapped, the aged, etc.—I feel that you will understand my wishing to discuss the current status of Intro One with you. . . .

This legislation has been tied-up in the General Welfare Committee and not been permitted to go before the full Council—a situation tantamount to the filibustering in the U.S. Congress that succeeded from 1876-1964 in frustrating the will of the Congress by not permitting the Civil Rights Bills to go to the floors of the House and Senate.

In light of this unhappy and long experience which did grave damage to blacks in our society, I would urge you . . . to vote for a discharge motion that would make it possible for the full Council to act. . . .

I should appreciate hearing from you regarding this matter.

Sincerely,

Bayard Rustin

*   *   *

"Bayard Rustin's Statement on Proposed Amendments to Law Banning Discrimination on the Basis of Sexual Orientation" (April 17, 1986)

Rustin opposed amendments designed to weaken the New York City Gay Rights Law, arguing that "history demonstrates that no group is ultimately safe from prejudice, bigotry, and harassment so long as any group is subject to special negative treatment."

April 17, 1986

I am Bayard Rustin, Chairman of the Randolph Institute and Chairman of the Executive Committee of the Leadership Conference on Civil Rights which is composed of over 150 national groups dedicated to human rights for all. As one who has been active in the struggle to extend democracy to all Americans for over 50 years I am opposed to any attempt to amend the recently enacted law banning discrimination on the basis of sexual orientation.

I have been arrested 24 times in the struggle for civil and human rights. My first arrest was in 1928 merely for distributing leaflets on behalf of Al Smith's candidacy for President in a climate of anti-Catholic hysteria. Since that time I have fought against religious intolerance, political harassment and racism both here and abroad. I have fought against untouchability in India, against tribalism in Africa, and have sought to ensure that refugees coming to our shores are not subject to the same types of bigotry and intolerance from which they fled. As a member of the U.S. Holocaust Memorial Council I have fought anti-Semitism not only in the United States but around the world.

On the basis of such experiences, I categorically can state and history reveals that when laws are amended to provide "legal loopholes" that deny equal protection for any group of citizens, an immediate threat is created for everyone, including those who may think they are forever immune to the consequences of such discrimination. History demonstrates that no group is ultimately safe from prejudice, bigotry, and harassment so long as any group is subject to special neg-ative treatment. The only final security for all is to provide now equal protec-tion for every group under the law.

I therefore call upon all New Yorkers to give this new law a chance before considering any revisions.

I call upon the City Council to reject amendments to the law that would deny to lesbians and gay men protections that are enjoyed by all other citizens.

I call upon Mayor [Edward] Koch to veto any amendments designed to weaken this law should such amendments be passed.

~

Bibliographic Essay

The Bayard Rustin Papers contain a host of primary material on Rustin's life and work. They are housed at the Library of Congress in Washington, D.C.; a microfilm edition is available from University Publications of America, 4520 East-West Highway, Bethesda, MD 20814-3389. *A Guide to the Microfilm Edition of the Bayard Rustin Papers* (Bethesda, MD: University Publications of America, 1988) gives details of the papers' contents.

John D'Emilio, *Lost Prophet: The Life and Times of Bayard Rustin* (New York: Free Press, 2003) is a complete, recent biography that places needed emphasis on the ways in which Rustin's homosexuality shaped his life and career. Other useful biographies include Daniel Levine, *Bayard Rustin and the Civil Rights Movement* (New Brunswick, NJ: Rutgers University Press, 2000), and Jervis Anderson, *Bayard Rustin: Troubles I've Seen* (New York: HarperCollins, 1997). "Brother Outsider: The Life of Bayard Rustin" (DVD, directed by Nancy Kates and Bennett L. Singer, South Burlington, VT: California Newsreel, 2002) is an excellent documentary treatment that focuses on how this "Shadow Man" profoundly influenced mainstream American institutions. Two collections of Rustin's writings are especially useful: *Down the Line* (Chicago: Quadrangle Books, 1971) and Devon W. Carbado and Donald Weise, *Time on Two Crosses: The Collected Writings of Bayard Rustin* (San Francisco: Cleis Press, 2003). Rustin also published *Strategies for Freedom: The Changing Patterns of Black Protest* (New York: Columbia University Press, 1976).

Useful biographies and autobiographies of Rustin's contemporaries include Paula F. Pfeffer, *A. Philip Randolph: Pioneer of the Civil Rights Movement* (Baton Rouge: Louisiana State University Press, 1996); Andrew E. Kersten, *A. Philip*

Randolph: A Life in the Vanguard (Lanham, MD: Rowman & Littlefield, 2007); David J. Garrow, *Bearing the Cross: Martin Luther King, Jr. and the Southern Christian Leadership Conference* (New York: William Morrow, 1986); David Levering Lewis, *King: A Critical Biography* (New York: Praeger, 1970); Nat Hentoff, *Peace Agitator: The Story of A.J. Muste* (New York: Macmillan, 1963); Roy Wilkins and Tom Mathers, *Standing Fast: The Autobiography of Roy Wilkins* (New York: Viking Press, 1982); Malcolm X and Alex Haley, *The Autobiography of Malcolm X* (New York: Grove Press, 1965); Nancy J. Weiss, *Whitney M. Young, Jr. and the Struggle for Civil Rights* (Princeton, NJ: Princeton University Press, 1989); John Lewis and Michael D'Orso, *Walking with the Wind* (New York: Simon & Schuster, 1998); Richard D. Kahlenberg, *Tough Liberal: Albert Shanker and the Battle Over Schools, Unions, Race, and Democracy* (New York: Columbia University Press, 2007); Nelson Lichtenstein, *The Most Dangerous Man in Detroit: Walter Reuther and the Fate of American Labor* (New York: Basic Books, 1995); Maurice Isserman, *The Other American: The Life of Michael Harrington* (New York: Public Affairs, 2000); W. A. Swanberg, *Norman Thomas: The Last Idealist* (New York: Scribner, 1976); Clarence Taylor, *Knocking at Our Own Door: Milton A. Galamison and the Struggle to Integrate New York City Schools* (New York: Columbia University Press, 1997); Andrew F. Smith, *Rescuing the World: The Life and Times of Leo Cherne* (Albany: State University of New York Press, 2002) (Cherne served as head of the International Rescue Committee).

The historical literature on the civil rights movement that Rustin did so much to shape is vast. Essential general works include Taylor Branch's three-volume study of what he aptly labels "The King Years," from 1954 to 1968: *Parting the Waters* (New York: Simon & Schuster, 1988), *Pillar of Fire* (New York: Simon & Schuster, 1998), and *At Canaan's Edge* (New York: Simon & Schuster, 2006). Robert Weisbrot, *Freedom Bound: A History of America's Civil Rights Movement* (New York: Norton, 1990), and Harvard Sitkoff, *The Struggle for Black Equality, 1954–1980* (New York: Hill and Wang, 1981), are comprehensive one-volume treatments. Henry Hampton and Steve Fayer, *Voices of Freedom: An Oral History of the Civil Rights Movement from the 1950s through the 1980s* (New York: Bantam Books, 1990), contains interviews with a wide array of movement participants, including Rustin.

Two essential books for understanding race and civil rights in the 1960s and 1970s are Nicholas Lemann, *The Promised Land: The Great Black Migration and How It Changed America* (New York: Knopf, 1991), which interweaves the story of the planning and implementation of Great Society programs with personal stories of the struggles of African Americans for better lives in the ghettos of the North; and J. Anthony Lukas, *Common Ground: A Turbulent Decade in the Lives of Three American Families* (New York: Knopf, 1985), which employs the battle over court-ordered busing in Boston to explore the interconnections of race and class in America. William J. Wilson, *The Declining Significance of Race: Blacks and Changing American Institutions* (Chicago: University of Chicago Press, 1978), expresses Rustin's view that economic dislocation, not overt racism, was the major cause of black poverty in the 1960s and 1970s. Thomas Sugrue, *The Origins of the Urban Crisis: Race and Inequality in Postwar Detroit* (Princeton, NJ: Princeton University Press, 1996), also echoes Rustin by tracing the roots of urban decline to deindustrialization and job flight in the decades following World War II, as well as to the determination of white property owners, abetted by federal policies, to maintain residential segregation.

Rustin's life intersected with virtually every major event, theme, and moment of the modern civil rights movement. Herbert Garfinkel examines the 1941 March on Washington Movement in *When Negroes March: The March on Washington Movement in and the Organizational Politics for FEPC* (Glencoe, IL: Free Press, 1959); Lucy Barber, *Marching on Washington: The Forging of an American Political Tradition* (Berkeley: University of California Press, 2002), shows how marches on the nation's capital have affected the culture of protest in the United States. Marian Mollin, "The Limits of Egalitarianism: Radical Pacifism, Civil Rights, and the Journey of Reconciliation," *Radical History Review*, 88 (Winter 2004): 113–38, contains a critical analysis of the nonviolent direct action campaign in which Rustin played a major role. Richard M. Dalfiume discusses Randolph and Rustin's campaign to integrate the American military in *Desegregation of the U.S. Armed Forces: Fighting on Two Fronts, 1939–1953* (Columbia: University of Missouri Press, 1969). Richard Kluger, *Simple Justice: The History of* Brown v. Board of Education *and Black America's Struggle for Equality* (New York: Knopf, 1976), and James T. Patterson, Brown v. Board of Education: *A Civil Rights Milestone and Its Troubled Legacy* (Oxford and New York: Oxford University Press, 2001), examine the case that began the modern civil rights movement. Martin Luther King, Jr.'s *Stride Toward Freedom: The Montgomery Story* (New York: Harper, 1958) provides a first-person account of the Montgomery bus boycott, while Stewart Burns, *Daybreak of Freedom: The Montgomery Bus Boycott* (Chapel Hill: University of North Carolina Press, 1997), is the standard scholarly historical treatment. Raymond Arsenault's *Freedom Riders: 1961 and the Struggle for Racial Justice* (New York: Oxford University Press, 2006) discusses the effort to desegregate Southern bus transportation that owed so much to Rustin and the Journey of Reconciliation. King's Birmingham movement is the subject of Diane McWhorter's *Carry Me Home: Birmingham Alabama, The Climactic Battle of the Civil Rights Revolution* (New York: Simon & Schuster, 2001), a moving personal account by a white observer that combines memoir and history. A critical view of President Kennedy's cautious approach to civil rights is presented in Nick Bryant, *The Bystander: John F. Kennedy and the Struggle for Black Equality* (New York: Basic Books, 2006).

The March on Washington may be the single most written-about event of the modern civil rights movement. Drew Hansen, *The Dream: Martin Luther King, Jr. and the Speech that Inspired a Nation* (New York: Ecco, 2003), contains a textual analysis of the "Dream" speech, and a discussion of the different ways in which it has been interpreted over the years. Hampton and Fayer, *Voices of Freedom*, and Patrik Henry Bass, *Like a Mighty Stream: The March on Washington, August 28, 1963* (Philadelphia: Running Press, 2002), offer useful oral histories. John Lewis and Michael D'Orso discuss his controversial March on Washington speech in his autobiography, *Walking with the Wind*. Michael Eric Dyson, *I May Not Get There With You: The True Martin Luther King, Jr.* (New York: Free Press, 2000), argues for a more radical reading of King's public statements that emphasizes his commitment to economic and social equality in the United States. Branch, *Parting the Waters*, and Garrow, *Bearing the Cross* both contain narrative accounts of the March on Washington. Nick Kotz, *Judgment Days: Lyndon Baines Johnson, Martin Luther King, Jr., and the Laws that Changed America* (Boston and New York: Houghton Mifflin, 2005), examines the historic collaboration that produced the Civil Rights Act of 1964 and the Voting Rights Act of 1965. Stokely Carmichael and Charles V. Hamilton, *Black Power: The Politics of Liberation in America* (New York: Random House, 1967), explain the doctrine introduced by Carmichael in 1966.

Hugh Davis Graham, *The Civil Rights Era: Origins and Development of National Policy, 1960-1972* (New York: Oxford University Press, 1990), discusses the growth of affirmative action programs during the Kennedy, Johnson, and Nixon administrations. The Memphis sanitationmen's unionization campaign in which Martin Luther King, Jr., was participating at the time of his death is the subject of Michael Honey's *Going Down Jericho Road: The Memphis Strike, Martin Luther King's Last Campaign* (New York: W. W. Norton, 2007). The *Report of the National Advisory Commission on Civil Disorders* (New York: Bantam Books, 1968), popularly known as the Kerner Report, examines the causes of the racial disturbances of the mid-1960s and offers a recommendation—disregarded by President Johnson—for a massive expansion of government-sponsored antipoverty programs in the nation's ghettos.

Useful books on the Ocean Hill-Brownsville controversy include Jerald Podair, *The Strike that Changed New York: Blacks, Whites, and the Ocean Hill-Brownsville Crisis* (New Haven: Yale University Press, 2002); Daniel H. Perlstein, *Justice, Justice: School Politics and the Eclipse of Liberalism* (New York: Peter Lang, 2004); and Jane Anna Gordon, *Why They Couldn't Wait: A Critique of Black-Jewish Conflict Over Community Control in Ocean Hill-Brownsville, 1967–1971* (New York: RoutledgeFalmer, 2001). Rustin's tortured choices during the Ocean Hill crisis are examined in Daniel H. Perlstein, "The Dead End of Despair: Bayard Rustin, the 1968 New York School Crisis, and the Struggle for Racial Justice," *Afro-Americans in New York Life and History*, 31 (July 2007): 89–121.

Useful histories of the major civil rights organizations include August Meier and Elliott M. Rudwick, *CORE: A Study in the Civil Rights Movement, 1942–1968* (New York: Oxford University Press, 1973); Clayborne Carson, *In Struggle: SNCC and the Black Awakening of the 1960s* (Cambridge: Harvard University Press, 1981); Wesley C. Hogan, *Many Minds, One Heart: SNCC's Dream for a New America* (Chapel Hill: University of North Carolina Press, 2007); and Adam Fairclough, *To Redeem the Soul of America: The Southern Christian Leadership Conference and Martin Luther King, Jr.* (Athens: University of Georgia Press, 1987).

The tensions between the civil rights and labor movements, which Rustin sought to resolve, are explored in Bruce Nelson, *Divided We Stand: American Workers and the Struggle for Black Equality* (Princeton, NJ: Princeton University Press, 2001) and Paul D. Moreno, *Black Americans and Organized Labor: A New History* (Baton Rouge: Louisiana State University Press, 2006).

Two influential pacifist texts that played a major role in the development of the philosophy of nonviolent direct action are Richard Gregg, *The Power of Nonviolence* (Philadelphia: J. B. Lippincott, 1934) and Krshnalala Sridharani, *War Without Violence: A Study of Gandhi's Method and Its Accomplishments* (New York: Brace and Company, 1939). Sudarshan Kapur, *Raising Up a Prophet: The African-American Encounter with Gandhi* (Boston: Beacon Press, 1992), discusses the Indian revolutionary's influence on the black community in the United States. James Tracy, *Direct Action: Racial Pacifism from the Union Eight to the Chicago Seven* (Chicago: University of Chicago Press, 1996), is a history of the movement that was one of the motivating forces of Rustin's life and career. The works of Rustin's pacifist mentor are collected in Nat Hentoff, ed., *The Essays of A.J. Muste* (Indianapolis: Bobbs-Merrill, 1967).

The obstacles Rustin faced in his lifelong crusade for economic justice in the United States are discussed in James T. Patterson, *America's Struggle Against Poverty in the Twentieth Century* (Cambridge: Harvard University Press, 2000). Michael Harrington, *The Other America: Poverty in the United States* (New York: Macmillan, 1962), written by Rustin's socialist ally, is credited with launching the War on Poverty. Charles A. Murray, *Losing Ground: American Social Policy, 1950–1980* (New York: Basic Books, 1984) offers a critical view of Great Society antipoverty policies, while Daniel Patrick Moynihan, *The Politics of a Guaranteed Income: The Nixon Administration and the Family Assistance Plan* (New York: Random House, 1973), ponders the ironies of a Republican president's attempt to realize Rustin's vision of a minimum income for every American.

John D'Emilio, *Sexual Politics, Sexual Communities: The Making of a Homosexual Minority in the United States, 1940–1970* (Chicago: University of Chicago Press, 1983), is an authoritative history of American gay identity. The gay environment that Rustin encountered when he moved to New York as a young man is described in George Chauncey, *Gay New York: Gender, Urban Culture, and the Makings of the Gay Male World, 1890–1940* (New York: Basic Books, 1994). Rustin discusses his sexuality in "An Interview with Bayard Rustin," in Redvers Jeanmarie, *Other Countries: Black Gay Voices*, Vol. 1 (New York: Other Countries Collective, 1988).

The mobilization in opposition to the war in Vietnam that so conflicted Rustin is examined in Charles DeBenedetti and Charles Chatfield, *An American Ordeal: The Antiwar Movement of the Vietnam Era* (Syracuse, NY: Syracuse University Press, 1990). Todd Gitlin, *The Sixties: Years of Hope, Days of Rage* (New York: Bantam Books, 1997), also contains a perceptive discussion of the antiwar movement. The origins of the New Left are analyzed in Maurice Isserman, *If I Had a Hammer: The Death of the Old Left and the Birth of the New Left* (New York: Basic Books, 1987), and the story of its most significant organization is told in Kirkpatrick Sale, *SDS* (New York: Random House, 1973). Peter B. Levy, *The New Left and Labor in the 1960s* (Urbana: University of Illinois Press, 1994), examines the uneasy relationship between radicals and workers that trapped Rustin and forced him to choose between elements of his American dream.

Mark Dawson, *Flight: Refugees and the Quest for Freedom, The History of the International Rescue Committee, 1933–1993* (New York: International Rescue Committee, 1993), is the official history of the organization to which Rustin devoted time and energy during the last decades of his life. See also Aaron Levenstein, *Escape to Freedom: The Story of the International Rescue Committee* (Westport, CT: Greenwood Press, 1983). Two recent volumes examine the campaign to liberate Soviet Jews that Rustin helped lead. See Stuart Altshuler, *From Exodus to Freedom: A History of the Soviet Jewry Movement* (Lanham, MD: Rowman & Littlefield, 2005) and Henry L. Feingold, *Silent No More: Saving the Jews of Russia, The American Jewish Effort, 1967–1989* (Syracuse, NY: Syracuse University Press, 2007).

Allen J. Matusow, *The Unraveling of America: A History of Liberalism in the 1960s* (New York: Harper & Row, 1984) and Gitlin, *The Sixties: Years of Hope, Days of Rage*, offer contrasting perspectives on the political and social movements of the decade. The essays in Steve Fraser and Gary Gerstle, *The Rise and Fall of the New Deal Order, 1930–1980* (Princeton, NJ: Princeton University Press, 1989), explore the achievements and failures of the New Deal–style liberalism that deeply influenced Rustin's politics and activism.

Index

~

About the Author

Jerald Podair teaches American history at Lawrence University, where he is the Robert S. French Professor of American Studies. He is the author of *The Strike That Changed New York: Blacks, Whites, and the Ocean Hill-Brownsville Crisis*, which was a finalist for the Organization of American Historians' Liberty Legacy Foundation Award for the best book on the struggle for civil rights in the United States, and an honorable mention for the Urban History Association's Book Award in North American urban history. He is the recipient of the Allan Nevins Prize, awarded by the Society of American Historians for "literary distinction in the writing of history."